LIVING LIGHTLY

NICOLA TURNER

The Busy Person's Guide to Mindful Consumption

HarperCollins*Publishers*

CONTENTS

HarperCollins*Publishers*

First published in 2020
by HarperCollins*Publishers* (New Zealand) Limited
Unit D1, 63 Apollo Drive, Rosedale, Auckland 0632, New Zealand
harpercollins.co.nz

Copyright © Mainstream Green Ltd 2020

HarperCollins*Publishers*

Unit D1, 63 Apollo Drive, Rosedale, Auckland 0632, New Zealand
Level 13, 201 Elizabeth Street, Sydney NSW 2000, Australia
A 53, Sector 57, Noida, UP, India
1 London Bridge Street, London, SE1 9GF, United Kingdom
Bay Adelaide Centre, East Tower, 22 Adelaide Street West, 41st floor,
    Toronto, Ontario M5H 4E3, Canada
195 Broadway, New York NY 10007, USA

A catalogue record for this book is available from
the National Library of New Zealand

ISBN 978 1 7755 4150 9 (pbk)

Cover and internal design by Megan van Staden
Creative direction and illustrations by Tori Veysey – Journeyman Creative
Cover photography by Sacha Kahaki (front) and Jodi Bennett (back)
Internal photography by Tori Veysey – Journeyman Creative, with the exception of the following pictures.
Jodi Bennett: pages 13, 14, 114, 126, 154, 164, 172, 196, 222 and 234; Sacha Kahaki: pages 2, 6, 46, 100, 140, 177, 201 and 225; and Pioneer studio: page 137. Photographs on pages 61, 70, 97, 116, 186, 210 and 214 were supplied by the subjects.
Typeset in Gazette, Neuzeit and Fajny

Colour reproduction by Splitting Image Colour Studio, Clayton VIC
Printed and bound in China by RR Donnelley

8 7 6 5 4 3 2 1   20 21 22 23 24

WHY A BOOK?

I love spreading the concept of mindful consumption by talking with people. There's nothing like the power of human to human interaction to engage and create change. But there's only so many places and people I can get to. I may not ever make it to where you are, or I might be in your town on a Wednesday night and you can't make it because it clashes with your Zumba class or the parent–teacher meeting. There's also a certain irony in flying and driving all over the place to talk about mindful consumption.

Over the years, I've had lots of people ask me to write a book. I wasn't that down with it because it just felt like I was creating more stuff and waste and it also sounded like a whole lot of hard work (I can now legit confirm that it is a heap of work). But, over time, I've reflected on our human connection with books. In what has become a hyper digital world, there's nothing like holding a book in your hands, flicking through the pages and inhaling the smell of paper (or is that just me?). It also means that I can engage with you about mindful consumption wherever you are and whenever suits you. If writing a book means more people are into living lightly then I reckon it's the right thing to do. Just know that I'm way funnier and better looking in real life.

I'm stoked to have a publisher who's fully on board with creating a book with less impact. Here's some of the good stuff that happened in the making of this thing:

- The book is printed on Forestry Stewardship Council (FSC) certified paper. ← *FSC is all about promoting responsible management of the world's forests.*
- All inks used are low VOC (volatile organic compounds), meaning they're way better from an ingredient perspective. Colour was used sparingly, and we avoided excessive coatings and finishes (luckily, high-gloss isn't really my style anyway).
- The printing plant is doing some amazing stuff around energy efficiency, including LED lighting, solar power and wastewater recycling. Any leftover materials such as excess paper, plastic and metal printing plates will be recycled.
- Reviewing and editing of the book was done almost entirely electronically.
- All of the props and clothes in the photos are mine or borrowed from friends (if mine were too manky).

As the reader, I would be pumped if you could reuse this book as much as possible and then pass it on when you're done with it or even donate it to your local library.

#Imperfectaction

TO BEGIN

'We don't need a handful of people doing Zero Waste perfectly. We need millions of people doing it imperfectly.'

– ANNE MARIE BONNEAU

I really want to do what's right for the planet.

I totally get that the way we're living and consuming is not sustainable, and we all need to be doing our bit.

But, if I'm really honest with myself (the type of honest you are when nobody is looking), I know I'm only going to change my behaviour if it works for me. Life is busy; change is only going to happen if it's not going to take too much time, cost too much money, or turn me into a weirdo who no longer gets invited to cool parties.

Bottom line – I'm only going to live more sustainably if it doesn't compromise my lifestyle.

> **So, what if I told you I've found a way:**
> - To reduce our impact within the juggle of our crazy-busy modern-day lives.
> - To keep it real with changes that actually save time and make life simpler.
> - To have a lighter mindset that's better for our own wellbeing and the wellbeing of the planet.

About me

I'm a suburban mum of two young children; I have a day job, a husband and a vague social life – life is pretty busy. We're what I'd consider to be a pretty typical household, juggling life in a pretty typical way.

Over the past 7 years, we've been on a journey to simplify the way we live, to drop a speed on the treadmill of life and to lighten our impact on the world around us. It's been about being more mindful of how we're consuming and it has staggered me how much better it's been for our wellbeing, and the planet's wellbeing too.

The best thing about the changes we've made is that it hasn't meant going without or sacrifice. In fact, life has become better in so many ways, and we've managed to significantly decrease our footprint on the earth. Bonus.

It's been such an epic shift for us with so many upsides that I couldn't shake the need to spread the message far and wide. I've spent the last five years fusing my personal journey with my previous career experience, and am now stoked to work with businesses, councils and individuals to spread the word about mindful consumption.

About the book

To share what I've learned from my adventure, to show that living lightly with less impact is a game that everyone can play, I decided to write this book. I want to normalise mindful consumption and to create a shift in our collective mindset.

How I roll is not a gold standard approach, but it's what works for us within the realities of our family day to day. It's not intended to be a blueprint but, rather, a dose of inspiration to help you navigate your own way within your already busy life.

The book begins with my own journey to mindful consumption. I haven't always been this way, in fact life has done a 180 – and you'll realise that if I can do it, anyone can. Then, I dive into why this whole consumption thing is a big deal not only for the world around us but, also, for our own personal wellbeing. If you're like me, you'll feel a subtle shift in your thinking around the way we're living and consuming and realise that maybe it's not quite as convenient as we think. As all the cool kids say, you'll be 'woke'.

As we explore changing our habits, I'll share some of my favourite hacks for how to navigate behaviour change. We're human, which means we're complex and a bit niggly when it comes to change – having a toolbox of shortcuts will give you an awesome head start on your own adventure.

With the practical stuff, I've structured the book around the key areas in life where we've made changes. For simplicity, I've split the content into the two main areas of 'waste' and 'stuff', but things overlap, loop round and connect throughout all of the sections. Everything is connected.

Each of the practical chapters covers the things we do in our lives and is designed to give you a new mindset, as well as actionable ideas of changes you could make. I've even split each section into 'The mindset' and 'Getting it done' to help you find your way.

To wrap things up, I cover how to bring other people with you on the journey. Kids, partners, friends, work mates … Things go a whole lot smoother if you bring them on the ride instead of wildly throwing change at them.

Learn from my mistakes on this one!

Using the book

Use this book however works for you. I want it to create change; there's no judgement on how you make that happen.

You could:
- Go 'old school' and read it cover to cover.
- Choose your own adventure and jump around the sections that interest you.
- Flick through the images.
- Read one thing that resonates with you, then put it down and make one small change.
- Flip through the pages, find the Time Hacks and start with those. I've panned the gold for all of you extra busy humans – you're welcome!
- Share the love and pass the book on.
- Take photos of the pictures and text them to your mates.
- Leave it open at a relevant section on the coffee table when your mother-in-law is visiting.

Whether you know it or not, your journey has started just by picking up this book, and I'm stoked. Enjoy the ride.
– Nic

I HAVEN'T ALWAYS BEEN THIS WAY

'Life is trying things to see if they work.' – **RAY BRADBURY**

I'm a planner, I always have been. Strangely, when it came to my career, however, there was no planning involved. I just kind of fell into it.

It was 1999; the euro had just been created, the Backstreet Boys were breaking album sales records and I was wearing too much beige linen.

I was at university and needed a holiday job. Glossy clipart posters advertising summer internships started appearing around campus.

I went along to a presentation and was welcomed by stylish young people in boot-cut suits. They talked about career paths, professional development and future proofing. Their convincing words flowed out in what I would later learn was a tried-and-tested sales formula. It worked. I was sold.

I love writing lists for the pure satisfaction of ticking them off.

After a lengthy process of personality profiling, interviews and logic testing, I was considered logical and personable enough to be accepted into the fold. I spent the summer earning good coin and hanging out with smart, successful people. The internship led to the offer of a graduate position, and I fell into a 15-year career.

I worked in the Fast Moving Consumer Goods industry (FMCG). Despite the majority of the population having never heard of this term (it's the industry behind all those everyday products we buy regularly and consume frequently – think shampoo, baked beans, toilet paper and wine), we interact with it on a daily basis.

My job became understanding how we, as shoppers, behave in the supermarket. The way we move around the store (yep, there's traffic flow in a supermarket) and what we see, hear, smell and think. Ultimately, it's about understanding what makes us buy or not buy.

Huge amounts of science and research go into every shopper's move and notion. Globally, there is an army of people working to understand how we think and behave, with the goal of influencing us to consume more.

Insights come from the massive amount of data captured every time we tap a card, as well as focus groups, surveys and interviews. There are even shop-alongs, where willing people are paid to be observed and questioned throughout their shopping process. This involves sitting with them beforehand, in their home, as they write their shopping list, then following them around a store with a clipboard. 'Just pretend we're not here', we'd say. It was fascinating but very, very weird.

Virtual reality shopping labs are also a thing. People are paid to come in and experience a digital shopping environment where various scenarios can be tested. Eye-tracking glasses are used to determine where we look on the shelves, and heat maps are created showing the ideal place to put your product. What packaging colours and shapes draw our eyes, how wide the aisles should be to encourage us to browse more, what music should be playing in the store, where should the milk be ... every single product interaction is analysed to the extreme. The more insight and understanding there is about how we behave, the more things can be orchestrated to drive our consumption.

And here you thought you were innocently doing your weekly shop with your own free will.

There are pretty simple principles behind getting us to buy more:
- **Penetration** (yep, it always made me snigger in meetings): get more people buying the product
- **Frequency**: get people buying it more often
- **AWOP** (average weight of purchase): get people to pay more for it.

SUPERMARKET SMOKE AND MIRRORS

Here are some of the ways we're being influenced in the supermarket.

- Hitting the produce section first makes the store seem fresh and inviting, and makes us feel more upbeat. We start by filling our trollies with healthy food, which makes us feel better about loading it up with the not-so-healthy stuff later in the shop.

- It's no accident that the smell of rotisserie chicken and fresh bread wafts through the air at the beginning of our shopping journey – the hungrier we are, the more we tend to buy.

- We naturally default to looking at things between our hip and eye level, so that's where you'll find the products that retailers and suppliers most want us to buy.

- Products wanting to appeal to kids are placed at their eye level. It makes them easy to spot and cashes in on their 'pester power'.

- Large displays, moving products around, product sampling and advertising materials are in place to try to disrupt our shopping routine and get us to interact with and buy additional products.

- Different seasonal occasions are amped up in store to play on our human love of celebration – think big sporting events, Halloween, Easter, Mother's Day. Don't get me started on Christmas products hitting stores in September. Occasions are also conjured up to create interest and increase spending in stores – things like 'health and beauty' weeks or 'stock up your freezer' campaigns.

- Higher-margin impulse products are placed next to necessities to encourage purchasing – baby clothes and toys can be found right next to the nappies.

- Price promotions for buying multiple items increase our spend and play on the idea of expandable consumption – the more we have, the more we will consume. If I buy more potato chips, I'll eat more.

- Milk, butter, bread and other essentials are positioned at the back of the store, in the hope that we will be tempted by other things on the way through. High-volume, popular products are placed in the middle of the aisles to avoid the risk of the 'boomerang effect', where we don't go all the way down.

- The dulcet tones of elevator music fill our ears in the hope that it will make the shopping experience more enjoyable and slow us down so that we buy more.

- The temptation is real with magazines and sugary snacks at the checkout. Our waiting time turns into buying time – jackpot.

The standard model of the retail industry is based on increasing consumption – the more we buy and use, the better it is for business. The industry is good at what it does. Whether you're walking into a supermarket, a fashion retailer or a convenience store, an eye-watering amount of strategy and science has gone into your shopping experience. Combine that with the brand and product advertising that we're constantly surrounded by, and it's no wonder we've become wired to consume.

I never thought to question what I did; it's become the way of the world. My role was understanding human behaviour and it was fascinating.

I really liked my job. I was constantly learning. I got the salary, the car, the overseas travel and postings. I worked with very cool and exceptionally smart people. We worked hard and played hard. I felt like I was part of the 'in' club and was climbing that elusive ladder everyone talks about. I had this success thing all figured out.

Well, almost. If I really tuned in, there was always this niggling feeling that I was a fraud, that I didn't quite fit in. It was pretty easy to ignore, though; I was rolling with the wheels of progress.

But then something happened that started to change where those wheels were heading. I'd love to say it was some rock-star moment, a lightning bolt that shook me into a new way of being. I've even considered making something up, just to make it sound more impressive.

So, here it is. In 2011, my then-boyfriend Mike (he's still around, just upgraded to husband) started getting mild dermatitis on the index finger of his left hand. Yes, mild, and yes, one finger. That's the moment and the finger that changed the course of my career and lifestyle forever.

After a period of first-world annoyance, Mike headed off to the doctor and was given steroid cream to clear it up. And it did. In 48 hours, it was gone. Eureka. Except, then it came back. Over and over again.

It was a case of treating the symptoms and not the cause. Somewhere in the Rolodex of my mind was an article I'd read once, which claimed that, through the products we use, we put hundreds of synthetic chemicals on our skin every day.

As I started reading more about it, I found it had a name: toxic load. And I was now on a mission to reduce it. Chemistry was never my strong suit at school, but I understood enough to realise that we're only just beginning to comprehend the impact that some synthetic chemicals can have on ourselves and our planet. To me, it felt like the simplest and safest thing would be to just avoid them where we can.

And so, the journey began. We started a simple process of looking at the products we were using and questioning if we needed them. If we did, was there an alternative we could switch to that had simpler ingredients?

The product we used most frequently on our skin was hand soap, so we started there. We simply replaced our regular supermarket brand with a more natural alternative (→ for what we use, see page 118).

Mike's finger seemed grateful for the change and so we moved on to the next product. Every time we ran out of something, I'd apply the same process – do we need it, and if we do, is there a better choice?

Oh, before I continue – yes, he's okay. I've actually had people email me and ask me that question, so I wanted to put your minds at ease.

Of course, not all synthetic chemicals are bad – and not all natural chemicals are good. What's important is that we are more informed.

This wasn't some full-on assault that swept through our house, ridding it of every product with an unknown chemical name on the label. It was one small change at a time, where I questioned, simplified and made better choices.

I moved on from simplifying the products we were using on our skin, to those we used around us – our cleaning products. Then came the food that we were putting in us.

My motivation for change was driven by improving our own personal wellbeing – it was purely self-interest (I'm only human). But somewhere along the line, I realised that, by using fewer synthetic chemicals on ourselves, we were also doing better by the planet. That felt weirdly good.

> **THINGS JUST GET BETTER** By questioning each and every product we were using, we could simplify a LOT. It turns out, you don't need a different product for every room of the house and part of your body – who knew? By buying less, we were not only saving money but also reducing the amount of packaging waste we were creating. Fewer nasty chemicals, less cost and less waste … I felt like I'd hit the trifecta.

> ⊙ **TIME HACK** Simplifying the products you use means you're spending less time shopping for them, organising them and getting frustrated with cluttered drawers and cupboards.

At this point, I was feeling pretty pumped about the changes we'd already managed to make, which motivated me to keep going. I kept looking in our rubbish bin and finding new ways to reduce our waste. My mind began to move from looking at the everyday products we used in our home to all of the other stuff in our lives – furniture, clothes, kids' toys.

I jumped down that rabbit hole and started simplifying what we had and how we could break up with the constant quest for more.

While it didn't start that way, my journey now involves being mindful of everything we're consuming – from the food we're eating to the clothes we wear, and from the size of our house to the electricity we use. It's about buying and using less, and valuing things more. It's about living lighter.

It feels like, in our ever-busy lives, buying and consuming things is easy, convenient and controllable. It's become normalised and expected, it feels like it's the only way. Our consumption is pretty much running on autopilot.

With an already full life, I never wanted changing my consumption to become a new pastime, which filled my weekends and put pressure on my already time-poor week. My journey has been about reducing my family's impact in a way that doesn't take more time or effort, and that doesn't feel like we're going without. It's about rethinking the autopilot of consumption that we've fallen into and finding ways to do things better, all while managing the mother lode of daily life.

Seven-ish years and two kids later, we use at least 400 fewer synthetic chemicals in our home and on ourselves every day, we live with 10,000 fewer items (we have less stuff now than we did pre-kids) and we put out just one bag of rubbish a year.

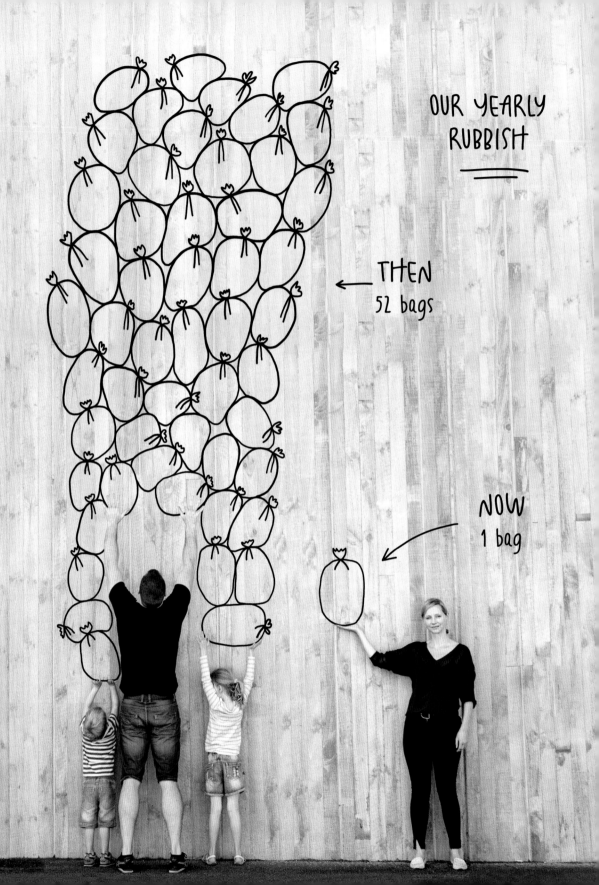

OUR YEARLY RUBBISH

← THEN
52 bags

NOW
1 bag

It seems counterintuitive, but we've actually saved a crazy amount of time and a heap of money. The best thing about it – we haven't had to compromise our lifestyle; in fact, it's got better. For real.

⊘ **TIME HACK** less stuff means fewer things to organise, tidy up and maintain.

Life has done a complete turn, and because we've done it one small change at a time, it hasn't hurt a bit.

I'm driven to create behaviour change in others. I always have been. I used to be about creating behaviour change to get people to consume more. Now, I'm about changing behaviour to get us to consume less. Same thing, different outcome.

I'm creating a movement where we're more mindful of how we consume and the waste we create. It's better for our own wellbeing and the wellbeing of the planet. Who's with me?

Life is simpler and, man, it feels good.

CONSUMPTION
– It's kind of a big deal

'We buy sh!t we don't need with money we don't have to impress people we don't like.' – VARIOUS

The way we are consuming is a big deal. What we're buying and the speed and scale that we're using things is proving too much for the planet. From the resources that go into the things we buy and use, to the waste we're left with afterwards – our consumption is our impact.

Then there's us – at face value, consuming seems harmless enough (hell, most of the time it feels good), but it's not all it's cracked up to be. For something we've been told makes our lives better and more convenient, it's taking up a shedload of our time and energy, and it has an enormous effect on our wellbeing.

> **FULL-ON STATS ABOUT CONSUMPTION**
> - According to *The Story of Stuff*, we're consuming twice as much as we did just 50 years ago.
> - It's estimated that every minute around the world, 1 million plastic bottles are being bought.
> - In my lifetime, the world's energy consumption has nearly doubled.

Consumption has become the way of the world. We even use GDP (Gross Domestic Product) as a measure of a country's success. The more stuff we buy and sell, the more successful we are considered to be.

Unless you're in Bhutan, which measures GNH (Gross National Happiness) – so freaken awesome.

I totally get why we consume more. There's so much choice for what we can spend our money on, and there's a massive industry convincing us that we need it. Then, of course, there's that hit we get when we buy something new – the instant gratification and surge of dopamine – which feels so darn good. It's what Freud called the 'pleasure principle' – as humans, we instinctively seek pleasure. It makes sense; buying things feels good and so we do more of it.

But while sales and GDP may look good on a graph, and that dopamine rush might give us a short-term buzz, the way we're consuming ain't all rainbows and unicorns.

Personal wellbeing

The scale and speed of our consumption has exploded over a really short period of time. It's easy to underestimate what a massive part of our lives it has become, and how much it impacts us.

More stuff, more time

I once heard that 'with every possession comes responsibility' – it's become a bit of a mantra. The more stuff we have, the more we have to look after, maintain, keep clean, organise, tidy up, get angry at our family for leaving out, move with and pass on to our kids when we die. The more stuff we have, the more responsibility we have, and the more time we spend on it. Studies also show that increased clutter can raise our cortisol and stress levels.

Having kids has made me hyper aware of how much of my life can be spent tidying things up and putting them away. Ideal Home in the UK published a survey that estimated we will spend 123 days of our lives sorting cupboards and wardrobes. Similarly, the act of getting older seems to have brought with it activities like needing to bring the outdoor furniture cushions inside at night time, cleaning the BBQ and sorting out my 'files'.

I'm all for taking responsibility for my stuff, but the less stuff I have, the less admin time I need to spend on it. Winning.

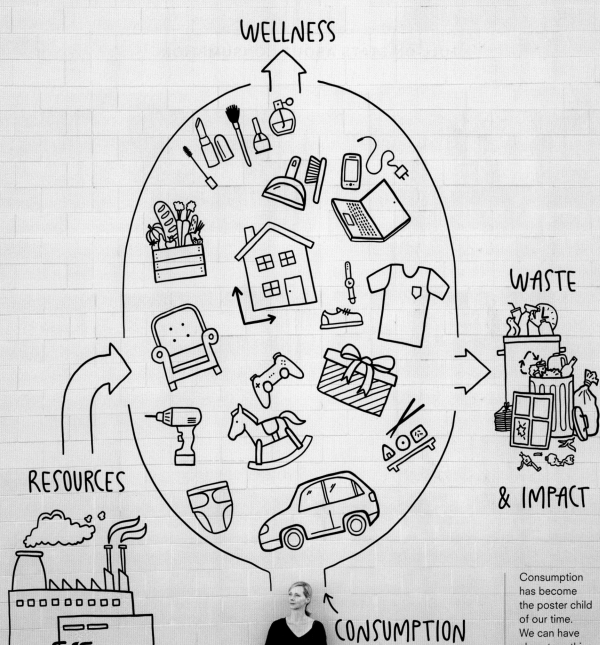

WELLNESS

WASTE

& IMPACT

RESOURCES

CONSUMPTION

How do we become more
mindful of how and
what we're consuming?

Consumption has become the poster child of our time. We can have almost anything imaginable, any time we want, and even delivered to our doorstep if we choose. We're buying and consuming more than ever before.

| ⊘ **TIME HACK** Having less stuff means less time
| doing 'admin' to look after it all.

Paradox of choice

When it comes to choice, it feels logical that 'more' should be more. But our brains can actually only process so much and it's really easy to get overwhelmed.

When I was in the supermarket game, we used to do shopper experiments with different shelf set-ups. One set-up would have, say, 100 different products on it and the second would have way fewer products. In the majority of cases, shoppers would feel like they had more choice with the second option – the one that had actually fewer choices. It seems counterintuitive, but it comes down to being able to navigate the shelf more easily. Less is easier on our brains.

It's part of the theory of the 'Paradox of Choice' (thanks to psychologist Barry Schwartz), which is the idea that the abundance of choice and options we have in our modern-day lives is not great for our wellbeing. We feel like we want choice, but too much of it can be overwhelming and exhausting.

It's having a crammed wardrobe but having 'nothing to wear'.

Those damn Joneses

Our society has this crazy tendency to judge people's success on what they have and what they consume. We measure each other on how much we have, and how big it is, how shiny and new. Moving up in the world normally means a bigger house, a later-model car and the newest sneakers.

When you stop and think about it, it seems almost laughable to judge people on the stuff they have and consume, instead of the people they are and the lives they live.

> ⊘ **TIME HACK** Letting go of the expectations of those judgey Joneses gives you more time to spend focusing on the type of life that suits you.

The myth of convenience

It can feel like buying things is the convenient answer in our time-poor lives, but there's a huge irony in how we're doing it. Driving past the rammed shopping mall carpark on the weekend, it can seem like shopping is our national sport. Between time at the mall, our multiple weekly trips to the supermarket, and those cheeky hours we spend scrolling shopping sites on the couch (while also double-screening by half-watching something on TV), we're spending a heap of time shopping for stuff. In fact, a study by OnePoll estimates that women spend an average of 8.5 years of their lives shopping. So much for convenience.

Of course, it feels good to get that hedonistic hit of the new shiny stuff. But once the new-car smell has faded and the dopamine has disbursed (and it does, surprisingly quickly), we're often just working harder to earn more money, or gathering more debt, to pay for the stuff and the bigger houses to fit it in.

I'm all for having comfort, convenience and appreciating nice things, but we need to find some balance in our constant quest for more. We need to move away from lives that are all about 'having' towards lives that are about 'being' and 'experiencing'. It's way more fun and way less time consuming.

NZ and Australia have some of the highest ratios of household debt to income.

Environmental wellbeing

We're part of something way bigger than ourselves. Like it or not, we can't exist without the environment we live in. We're not bigger or better than it, and we're not the top of the food chain. While it's a bit of a blow to the human ego, Mother Nature has the ultimate say in things. The way we're consuming must be doing her head in.

Three-nested-dependencies model

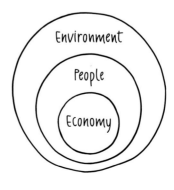

Environment · People · Economy

One of the big issues with the way we're consuming is that we've become really disposable.

How disposable are we?
- In North America, only 1% of the materials that are harvested, mined, processed and transported are still in use after six months. – *The Story of Stuff*
- Australian and Kiwi households throw out more than 1 tonne of waste every year.
- Every minute, about one rubbish truck-full of plastics is making its way into our oceans. – Ellen MacArthur Foundation
- Plastic is being found miles away from human habitation – it's in the air we breathe, the water we drink, the fish we're eating and the soil in which we're growing our food.

E.g., a plastic bag

We take oil from the ground (a finite natural resource)

We make it into a plastic bag (used, on average, for 6–12 mins)

We throw it away or it escapes into the environment.

Take – Make – Waste

Disposable consumption is often referred to as a 'linear' or 'Take – Make – Waste' approach.

Take

So much of what we're consuming comes from, or is reliant on, natural resources. We fill up our cars with petrol, buy things made and packaged in plastic made from oil, heat our water with natural gas, buy mobile phones made with precious metals …

There are no limits to how much we can consume, but there are very real limits on many of the resources that go into it.

Make

When we buy or consume things, it's easy to be out of touch with the impact that went into making and getting them to us. From the energy, resources and impact of the manufacturing process to the transportation to bring things to us – there's so much that occurs before our consumption, so much embedded impact. For every rubbish bin of waste we throw out, 70 bins of waste were made upstream to create what's in that one bin. Yep, 70! – The Story of Stuff

There's also often little thought given to the long-term impact of the materials that are used to make the products we consume, possibly made with ingredients that might be toxic to our own health and the health of the planet. According to The Story of Stuff, there are more than 100,000 different synthetic chemicals in commerce today.

Waste

When we throw things 'away', it's normally into a big old hole in the ground, which we call a landfill.

We throw all sorts of stuff in there, then pack it down really hard to the point where very little air gets in. This can then create a weird anaerobic environment where things don't break down normally like they would in nature. In a landfill, organic things (like banana peels and grass clippings) can break down in a way that creates methane – a greenhouse gas that's around 30 times more powerful than carbon dioxide.

Water can also permeate through a landfill, mix with all the funky things in there and create what's called 'leachate' (I like to call it 'rubbish juice'), which can make its way out into the environment and contaminate our soils and water.

Even though throwing things away might mean they're out of sight and out of mind, it doesn't mean they've disappeared. It's now thought that every piece of plastic ever made is still in existence. It might have broken down into tiny pieces (microplastics), but it's still there.

'There's no such thing as away.' – Annie Leonard

MICROPLASTICS = BIG DEAL Microplastics are a huge global issue – the sheer scale of them is mind blowing and they're getting everywhere, including into the food chain. Plastics have a crazy ability to act like a sponge for other toxins, and research is only just starting to understand the scale of the impact that microplastics are having on the health of us and our environment.

Changing the approach

We need to reconnect with the value of things – where they've come from and what happens to them. Instead of treating things as disposable, we need to use less and then keep reusing things over and over again. We need them to go around and around – what's called a 'circular' approach.

Nature is the perfect example of a circular approach where nothing is wasted. Something dies, falls to the ground and breaks down, creating nutrients for new growth.

Mother Nature has this stuff all figured out! Waste and rubbish are a human construct.

Linear

Take ⟶ Make ⟶ Waste

Circular

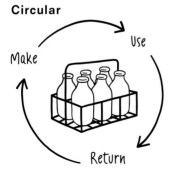

Make → Use → Return

Think glass milk bottles (or for the Kiwis, go with a good-old swappa crate).

Removes air to fit more rubbish and creates an anaerobic environment

METHANE

A strong greenhouse gas

Rubbish escapes into the environment.

LANDFILL

LEACHATE

AKA 'rubbish juice'

We've got the power

This is all great in theory and easy for me to write down, but changing the norms of consumption feels like a big ship to turn around, especially when we've all got our own stuff going on and lives to manage. It can be really tempting to just wait for someone else to fix it, right? It's easy to see this as something that the government and businesses need to sort out. They're not off the hook – they absolutely need to be doing everything they can but, it turns out, we have a heap of power as consumers. As Ruth Greenspan Bell put it, 'We need every tool in the toolbox, a big bag of human changes.'

We've got the power and we've also got the smarts. Of course, we need innovative people creating things like electric planes, packaging made from mushrooms and edible coffee cups – but there's no silver bullet, and technology is only part of the solution. We have everything we need right now to start making a difference, and the awesome news is that it doesn't have to be hard or time consuming.

Every single one of us has a role to play as tenants on this planet. As the Maori worldview conveys: our role is as kaitiaki, custodial guardians of the planet.

Let's go do this!

THE POWER OF US – PLASTIC BAGS IN NZ

Stage 1
Consumers (that's you and me) started getting pretty concerned about the impact plastic bags were having on our world. We'd seen the terrifying images of plastic bags clogging rivers and whales' bellies, and we were watching documentaries, signing petitions, talking about it on social media and shopping with our reusable bags.

Stage 2
Industry (e.g., the major supermarkets) recognised that plastic was a big concern for their customers. (Customer loyalty is kind of a big deal when you're in business.) So it became a race to be seen to be doing something about it. The two main supermarkets both got rid of single-use plastic bags and started charging for 'reusable' bags (also a smart business model).

Stage 3
The NZ government saw that plastic bags were a big deal to consumers (voters) and to industry (the supermarkets) and that bans were successfully happening in lots other states and countries around the world. On 1 July 2019, a single-use plastic shopping bag ban came into force in NZ (bans are already in place in most states in Australia).

The bag ban is not perfect, but it's a bloody good start. Due to consumer pressure, there's also now talk of banning plastic cotton buds, fruit stickers and more!

'We are the ones we've been waiting for.' – Alice Walker

MINDFUL CONSUMPTION

(when you don't have time)

*'Life is like underwear,
change is good.'* – UNKNOWN

This consumption thing is a big deal, both for us and the planet, and the power is in our hands to create change. But how do we go from 'knowing' to 'doing'? How do we start making changes when we're juggling the chaos of our already full lives?

It starts with accepting that we're human. That means we're complex, not always rational, and we're wired to take the path of least resistance.

To change our consumption habits, we need to embrace the realities of our behaviour and work with it to make changes.

AKA we're
a bit lazy.

THE MINDSET

Know why

Sure, I want to save the planet – but if I'm totally honest with myself, that's not enough to make me change. I'm also driven by the wellbeing of my family and saving time. Oh, and I'm not willing to compromise my lifestyle.

Time and simplicity have become my currency in life. Understanding this means I know what change needs to look like for it to work for me. It means that, when I nail a change in the right way, I'm way better off and I'm never going back.

Motivation is personal. You need to be honest with yourself – what lights your fire? It might be saving the turtles, simplifying your life, saving time, saving money, impressing your boyfriend or looking cool. Whatever it is – just own it.

Write it down, if that's your thing. Hell, you could even do a vision board – just know what your motivation is. Pause and think about it right now.

If you're anything like me, once you start making changes, you'll get hooked on the feeling of making a difference. Man, it feels good.

It may sound greedy, but it's honest.

> ⊘ **TIME HACK** If you know why you want to make changes, you'll spend less time mucking around with solutions that don't suit you and aren't going to stick.

Shift your mindset

We often consume on autopilot. If we need or want something, we go out and buy it or use it. If we're finished with it, we throw it away.

The single biggest change we can make to the way we consume is to become more conscious. Yep, that's it. That subtle shift in our mindset changes everything. Surely no one is too busy to do that!

Taking a micropause before we buy something allows us to ask, 'Do I really need or want this? And if I do, is there a way I can make a better choice?'

There are tons of ways we can make a better choice, but it starts with a pause and a conscious decision.

> ⊘ **TIME HACK** You'll figure out you don't need half the stuff you thought you did. You'll get back a heap of time from not having to think about it and shop for it.

> **KEEPING IT CONSCIOUS** Greenfulness™ is about being mindful of how we're consuming and the waste we're creating. It's breaking our autopilot consumption to take a mental micropause so we make conscious choices that are better for us and the planet.

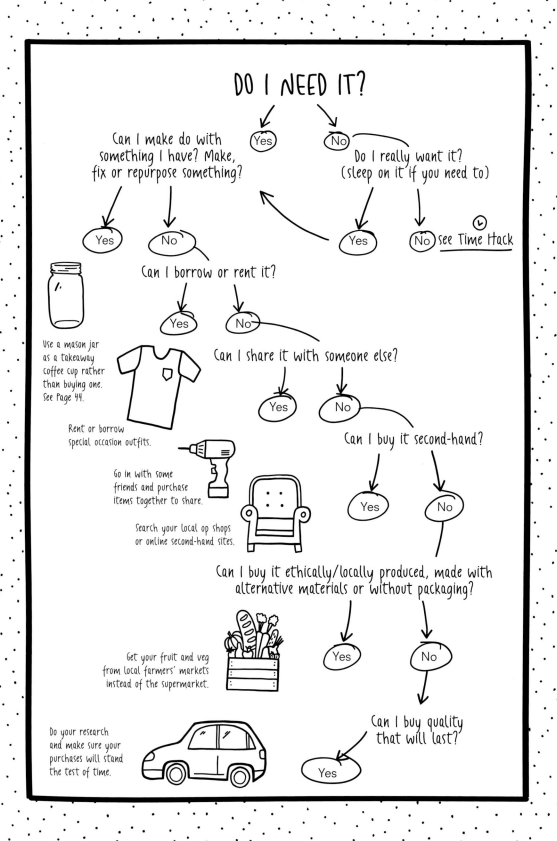

DO I NEED IT?

Yes

No

Do I really want it?
(sleep on it if you need to)

Yes

No — see Time Hack

Can I make do with something I have? Make, fix or repurpose something?

Yes

No

Can I borrow or rent it?

Yes

No

Use a mason jar as a takeaway coffee cup rather than buying one. See Page 44.

Rent or borrow special occasion outfits.

Can I share it with someone else?

Yes

No

Go in with some friends and purchase items together to share.

Search your local op shops or online second-hand sites.

Can I buy it second-hand?

Yes

No

Can I buy it ethically/locally produced, made with alternative materials or without packaging?

Yes

No

Get your fruit and veg from local farmers' markets instead of the supermarket.

Can I buy quality that will last?

Yes

Do your research and make sure your purchases will stand the test of time.

GETTING IT DONE

One small change

When we want to change the way we're consuming in our busy lives, it can be so easy to feel overwhelmed and then do nothing. The cool news is that this isn't an all-or-nothing game – making one tiny change is off-the-charts better than doing nothing.

The secret is to choose *something*, no matter how small (the smaller and easier, the better), and give it a whirl (one small change at a time also means you'll avoid freaking out your family or work mates).

Once you make a change, it will feel awesome and you'll be way more likely to go on and make more changes – that's what people call a 'gateway behaviour'.

I get that, sometimes, it can feel like, as one person making one small change, we're not going to make a dent in the universe. But it's small changes that have got us to this point – we haven't always consumed this way. In a bit over one generation, we've completely changed the way we consume. There was no dramatic lightning bolt; it's just been a slow and steady evolution of people consuming more. So we need to flip it into reverse so we have an evolution back to consuming less. Change happens because of the collective impact of people like you and me.

We started by changing our hand soap, and now we drive an electric car – just saying.

COLLECTIVE IMPACT

I live in a small town that, at last official count, has a population of 19,150 people. If everyone here switched to using bamboo toothbrushes and composted them, we would keep nearly 80,000 plastic toothbrushes out of landfill every year. Small changes multiplied.

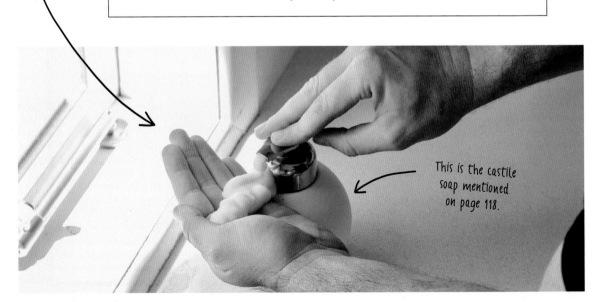

This is the castile soap mentioned on page 118.

Waste-free ice cream
= have it in a cone!

Keeping it real

There's no one-size-fits-all approach when it comes to making changes to our consumption. There's no sustainability rulebook that says we all have to toil in our gardens all weekend, preserve cumquats and whittle curios from foraged wood. I've learned to make changes that suit me and my lifestyle. If things are too hard, or take too long, they're not going to stick, so I find something that will. Changes don't have to be perfect (there's no such thing) – if I can move to something that's 'better', then I'm down with that. Don't let perfect be the enemy of good.

| ⊘ **TIME HACK** If you go with changes that suit you, they'll stick.

Imperfect action

When I first started on this journey, I was on parental leave. After immersing myself in blogs, books and Facebook groups about sustainability, I felt like I needed to start making things. I began making my own hand soap, dishwashing liquid, laundry detergent and more.

From a sustainability perspective, it was gold standard – no packaging, simple ingredients, low cost. But there was a slight problem … it took too long and I hated doing it. I've frequently tried to channel my inner Martha Stewart (the making Martha, not the prison one), but I don't find joy in making things.

I'd dread every time I ran out of something, and would even get p!ssed off with my husband if he was using too much of something!

Just because I wasn't into the 'ideal' solution, surely there were other choices I could make that were still good?

Turns out, there were …

Now, I buy brands where I know and trust the ingredients. I buy in bulk to save time and I refill my existing containers (→ see 'The bulk food store', page 79) when they eventually run out.

Fewer nasty chemicals, less packaging waste, time and money. Winning.

It's a solution that suits me and my very short attention span.

It's a change that feels good. Simple as.

We don't all live in an off-grid Instagram-worthy show home. We have day jobs, kids, unsupportive husbands (not you, Mike) and messy lives. Do what you can with where you're at, and don't feel guilty about the stuff that you can't fit in, or the things that go wrong.

LET IT GO Things don't always go to plan and that's okay. Sometimes, you'll forget your reusable coffee cup, buy too much at Kmart or drive your car to the shop up the road to get a bag of Twisties – feeling guilty about things doesn't help anyone, it just makes you feel stink. Have a laugh and let it go.

If you're into making stuff, then do it. And if you're really into it, do it for your mates as well – they'll welcome the time saving.

BELIEVE IN RIPPLES

If you ever feel like making one small change in your busy life isn't going to have an impact, I have two words for you … ripple effect.

CASE STUDY: CASCADING COFFEE CUPS

I had a friend come and stay with me from out of town. Her name is Amy and she is very tall (fake name and the tall thing is totally irrelevant to the story).

We went out for coffee and, as we walked to town, she complimented my reusable glass cup. Turned out, they sold the same cups at the café we were going to.

She found one in just the right colour combination, bought it and took it back home with her. (She was purely motivated by the fact that it looked cool – all good, whatever works!)

She works in a fancy corporate office in the big city and is part of a regular gaggle that go out for a daily takeaway coffee. On her first day back, she took her reusable cup with her. This is what went down:

- Day 1 – A couple of the group took the mickey out of her for being a 'tree hugger' and saving the turtles.
- Day 2 – Nobody said anything.
- Day 7 – Two others in the group started using reusable cups.
- **Week 3 – Every single person in the group was using a reusable cup.**

People want to do the right thing, they just don't want to feel awkward about doing something differently. Just by doing your own thing, you'll be normalising it for others. As humans, we're often driven by social norms. People will see your behaviour then think 'I can do that.' It's the ripple effect of change – the real-life version of 'going viral'.

⊘ **TIME HACK** Super-charge your impact by inspiring others.

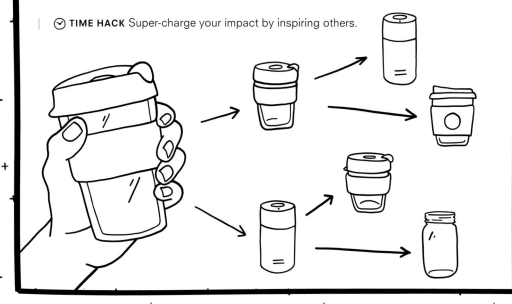

Change near you

I often have people ask me for a list of places where I shop. This might be useful if you live within a 2 km radius of my house, but otherwise, you're going to waste a whole lot of time (and petrol and money ...) travelling to places you don't need to. Create change where you are with the power of conversation (I know, in our modern-day world, talking to real people can feel a bit old school and awkward, but trust me on this one).

Here's a case in point. We get Indian takeaways.

Our local restaurant loves that we use our own containers, and I'm convinced it tastes better. We phone ahead and turn up 5 minutes earlier with our containers. Easy as.

Recently, we were heading to a friend's place out of town and decided to order takeaway from the local restaurant. This restaurant didn't know the drill.

Mike offered to make the call and have the conversation about bringing our own containers. He made the call from the bathroom so we weren't all listening. Fair enough.

A simple phone order ended up taking 10 minutes, as Mike explained that it was nothing against the containers that the restaurant used (didn't see that feedback coming) but, rather, us doing our bit to reduce waste.

It was a bit of a mission but, man, it was a powerful conversation.

They got it.

We used our own containers and, at pick up, the restaurant owner spent 20 minutes telling Mike how excited he was about encouraging his other customers to do the same thing – and he had even made a sign.

Our mates always take their own containers now.

Stoked.

Reality check – if you're dealing with a bigger organisation, you're not always going to get an immediate result. But you've planted a seed and, if enough people ask enough times, any customer-focused business with a few smarts will click onto the opportunity.

> ⊘ **TIME HACK** Creating change where you are means you don't have to waste time changing where you shop – make change happen around you.

Path of least resistance

I've read that the brain goes for the easiest thing first: the most obvious answer, the path of least resistance.

The day I admitted I was lazy was a breakthrough moment for making changes. If there's a shortcut to take, I'll take it. If there's an abridged version, I'm in. I'm not the only one – it's a human thing.

Acknowledging that I'll take the easy way out means that I need to make the good behaviour the easiest thing to do.

Sometimes, I'm amazed at how lazy I am and how ridiculous the shortcuts are that I take – but instead of fighting it, I've now learned to make tweaks to the process to redirect myself.

Despite having compost and worm bins, for instance, I tended to throw food scraps in the rubbish bin because it was 30 cm closer to me when I was standing at the sink – yep, 30 cm!

I swear takeaways taste better out of your own container.

I simply moved the compost and worm bins to be right next to the sink and put the rubbish bin in the cupboard under the sink. *Opening a door is such a drag.*

I even removed the rubber seals from the bench-top compost bins so they're easy and fast to open with one hand.

It's about creating a path of least resistance to the good behaviour. It's about figuring out what's stopping you from doing something and rejigging the process so it's fast and easy.

It's so simple, but trust me, it works.

⊘ **TIME HACK** Redesigning how you do things to make them as easy as possible will make life so much more efficient – who doesn't want that?

Share the load

We're all in our own bubble, busting our arses to manage the juggle of life. We're all trying to feed our families, stay on top of housework, make lunches, clothe ourselves, work ... and save the planet.

We often try and do and solve everything ourselves. We're all trying to do the same thing ... On our own.

It's ridiculously inefficient.

We often try and buy our way to convenience when it's already all around us. Managing the day-to-day isn't a competition. If we can make it easier, we all win.

⊘ **TIME HACK** Sharing the load with others means you can double-down on your resources.

WHAT IF WE SHARED THE LOAD?

- Let's say I want more home baking in my life:
  I could talk to a couple of my friends about each baking a bulk batch of something, then swapping it.
  Or maybe I have a friend who loves to bake:
  I could trade her baking for my time doing something else for her.
- Or I want to grow more vegetables:
  I could chat to my neighbours about each growing something different in our gardens, then swap.
- Or I have a neighbour who wants to start composting:
  We have heaps of space in our compost bin, so she could drop off her scraps once a week. She then keeps an eye on our place when we're away.
- Or my friend wants to buy more in bulk:
  When I'm next going to the bulk food shop, I could pick up a few things to get her started.

BURST YOUR BUBBLE Talking to people and asking them to do things can feel awkward in our insular modern-day world. Sometimes, I feel way more comfortable staying in my bubble and doing everything myself (and then complaining about how busy I am). But, every time I connect with someone and we nail a solution that works for both of us, it's the best freaken feeling!

Challenge convenience

When I was growing up, supermarkets were open standard business hours, 5½ days a week. The supermarket carpark on a Sunday was the go-to place to learn how to drive. Supermarkets are now open 7 days a week, if not 24 hours a day. It feels so much more convenient, right? We can go whenever we want. The problem is, because we can go whenever we want, we do. Most of us are shopping multiple times per week. The industry even has special names for all of the different types of shops we do – the main shop, the top-up shop, the special-occasion shop, the Friday-night shop, the dinner-tonight shop …

It feels like being able to have whatever we want, whenever we want, is a solution for our ever-busy lives – but because things are more convenient, we're able to be lazier with how we shop and, ironically, we're spending more time doing it.

Simplifying what I buy and how I shop for things has been the single biggest time-saving win I've made. Of course, sometimes 'popping to the shop' is the easiest and quickest thing to do, but I'm constantly surprised at how often it's not. Before I default to heading to the shops, I now take a pause and ask if there's another way.

> ⊘ **TIME HACK** Not leaving the house to go to the shop saves you a freaky amount of time.

Get political

I'm pretty introverted and don't even like commenting on social media. But here's how I 'get political' within my comfort zone:

- I sign petitions that are going to help reduce waste and move towards a circular economy – things like container deposit schemes (where you get money back for returning items like drink bottles – this gives the bottles a value, which increases recycling rates and keeps the bottles in circulation) and government-led product stewardship initiatives (programs that create responsibility for a product's end of life).
- At election time, I look into the environmental policies of the different political parties.
- I understand what my local council is doing about waste and sustainability, and give feedback through the submission process.
- I spend my money with companies that are doing good stuff, and offer feedback if it's not so good.

No showing off Aussies, you guys are all over this already. NZ is also starting to kick off.

⊘ **TIME HACK** Okay, so reading political policies might not save time, but find a mate who has already read them. The more political focus we have on sustainability, the more scale there is and the easier it makes it for everyone.

NIC'S TAKE: MOVING PAST ECO-ANXIETY

In one of my more intellectual evening viewing sessions, I watched the brilliant Al Gore documentary *An Inconvenient Sequel*. I'm not a hugely emotional person, but I shed a tear. I was completely overcome by how bad the state of the planet is and that, as humans, it's all our fault.

I guess I had a moment of eco-anxiety. Yep, it's an actual thing, and becoming more of a thing.

It's pretty easy to feel overwhelmed by the sheer scale of the challenge we're dealing with. It's BIG, it's the first time we've dealt with it and there's no silver bullet to solve it.

I have had more than one moment of eco-anxiety, and I'm sure there will be others. What I've realised, however, is that our power comes when we focus on what we can do, not how screwed we are. There are only so many images of dead birds with stomachs filled with plastic that my brain can deal with.

We need action, and making it happen feels good, so let's harness that. Let's focus on what's possible and surround and inspire ourselves with stories of good people doing good stuff.

There's so much power in people like us making small changes.

Eco-anxiety is 'the state of heightened anxiety some people experience relating to climate change.' – Honey Langcaster-James

⊘ **TIME HACK** Get on with the things you can change, rather than wallowing in how bad things are.

@ **FIND IT ONLINE** Check out websites like Auckland Council's livelightly.nz (such a great name) for simple, everyday actions you can take, inspirational stories, to make your own pledge of change and so much more.

A bit of accountability goes a long way.

Don't freak out about the state of things! Grab a cuppa and focus on what you can do.

I love the ritual and taste of loose-leaf tea – it also avoids any sneaky plastics or dodgy chemicals that can be in some teabags.

Homemade Lunchbox slice recipe on page 62

THE SKINNY ON WASTE

*'Waste is only waste
if we waste it.'* – will.i.am

What we throw out acts like a crystal ball into what we're consuming. Starting to reduce waste is a super-tangible way to tune into our consumption and to start making a difference.

I get it: when you're hauling your weekly rubbish to the kerb, or standing in front of a shop shelf deciding what to buy, it can feel like a big beast to tackle. Here are a few tools and insights to help you navigate the waters of waste without it taking over your life.

THE MINDSET

If you were a child of the '80s, you probably remember the mantra 'Reduce, reuse, recycle'. It's an awesome tagline, but things have evolved, and there are now a few more R words and they've been inserted into various versions of an inverted triangle. Think of it as a priority list of how to tackle waste. It's become something I subconsciously run through when I'm making choices.

The higher up the triangle you can get, further away from the pointy end, the better. Get high!

Hierarchy of waste

Here's my take on the waste hierarchy:

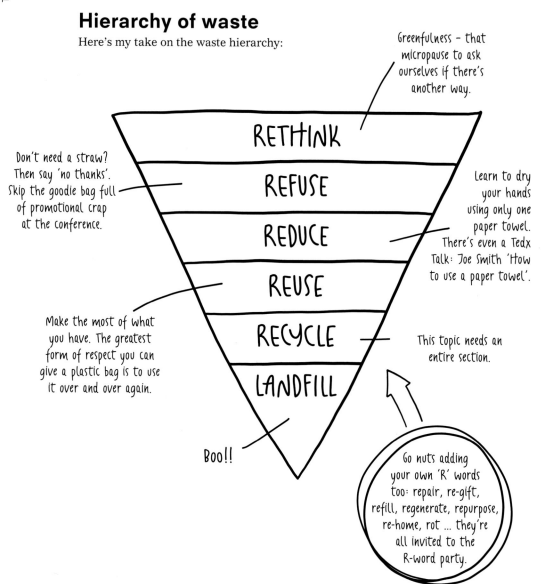

Greenfulness – that micropause to ask ourselves if there's another way.

Don't need a straw? Then say 'no thanks'. Skip the goodie bag full of promotional crap at the conference.

Learn to dry your hands using only one paper towel. There's even a Tedx Talk: Joe Smith 'How to use a paper towel'.

Make the most of what you have. The greatest form of respect you can give a plastic bag is to use it over and over again.

This topic needs an entire section.

RETHINK

REFUSE

REDUCE

REUSE

RECYCLE

LANDFILL

Boo!!

Go nuts adding your own 'R' words too: repair, re-gift, refill, regenerate, repurpose, re-home, rot ... they're all invited to the R-word party.

Recycling 101

I used to think, with my superior recycling diligence, I had this waste-reduction thing nailed. But, it turns out, recycling isn't quite the holy grail that I thought it was.

Supply and demand

Recycling is based on supply and demand. If there's value in the system, then it works; if there's not, it can get a bit messy.

Take plastics as an example

We're consuming way more plastics than anyone could have predicted. There's a whole lot of supply going into the system, without the right level of demand for the end product.

Not all plastics are created equal Some plastics can be recycled easily and repeatedly, but others not so much. Some types, such as soft plastics, often suffer from downcycling where the end product is a lower grade and has limited uses.

> Glass, steel and aluminium – these are great examples of materials that can be recycled over and over again.

A NOTE ON PLASTICS I'm not about demonising plastic – it's a bloody wonder material and has an important role to play in the world. I'm just not a fan of disposable or single-use plastic.

Leakage Just because things are recyclable doesn't mean it happens. The National Geographic Society estimated that only 9% of all plastics ever made have been recycled, and lots of it ends up in the environment.

Can we deal with it? Not having the right infrastructure to process materials locally means we can end up shipping them off to other countries to deal with. Sending shipping containers full of crappy low-grade plastics halfway around the world to be downcycled seems crazy.

Wishcycling Because we want things to be recyclable, we'll often end up putting things in our recycling bin that aren't actually recyclable – common offenders are coffee cups, plastic toys and plastic bags. Despite our good intentions, these products can end up contaminating the recycling, and may mean the whole batch goes to landfill. Check your local council's website to make sure you're getting it right.

The big picture

Time, energy and resources go into recycling. Even if something can be recycled, it still takes a heap of resources to make it. We'll use it for a short amount of time, then put it into our recycling bin. Someone comes along and collects, transports, sorts and processes it, and then transports it somewhere to (hopefully) be used again.

Recycling can be a good alternative to sending things to landfill, but it's complex. There are a whole lot of other actions further up the waste hierarchy that are a better choice. Ideally, we need to be shooting for buying and using less overall and keeping things in use for as long as we can.

Different approaches to using things

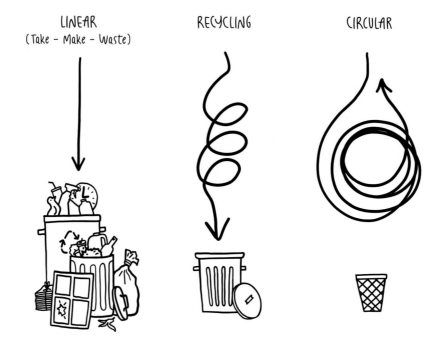

LINEAR
(Take – Make – Waste)

RECYCLING

CIRCULAR

GETTING IT DONE

For me, being more conscious of waste boils down to three simple questions:
1. **Do I need it?**
2. **How can I source it better?**
3. **What happens to it at the end of its life?**

Read on for more detail, but if you keep coming back to these questions, you'll be kicking goals.

Where to start

When I'm deciding what to do to reduce my waste, I use my rubbish bin as my guide (not my spiritual guide, that would be weird). Every time I'm ready to make a change, I look in my bin, see what's there and choose the next easiest thing to focus on.

It really doesn't matter where you start – just pick something, and make it an easy one to get you going.

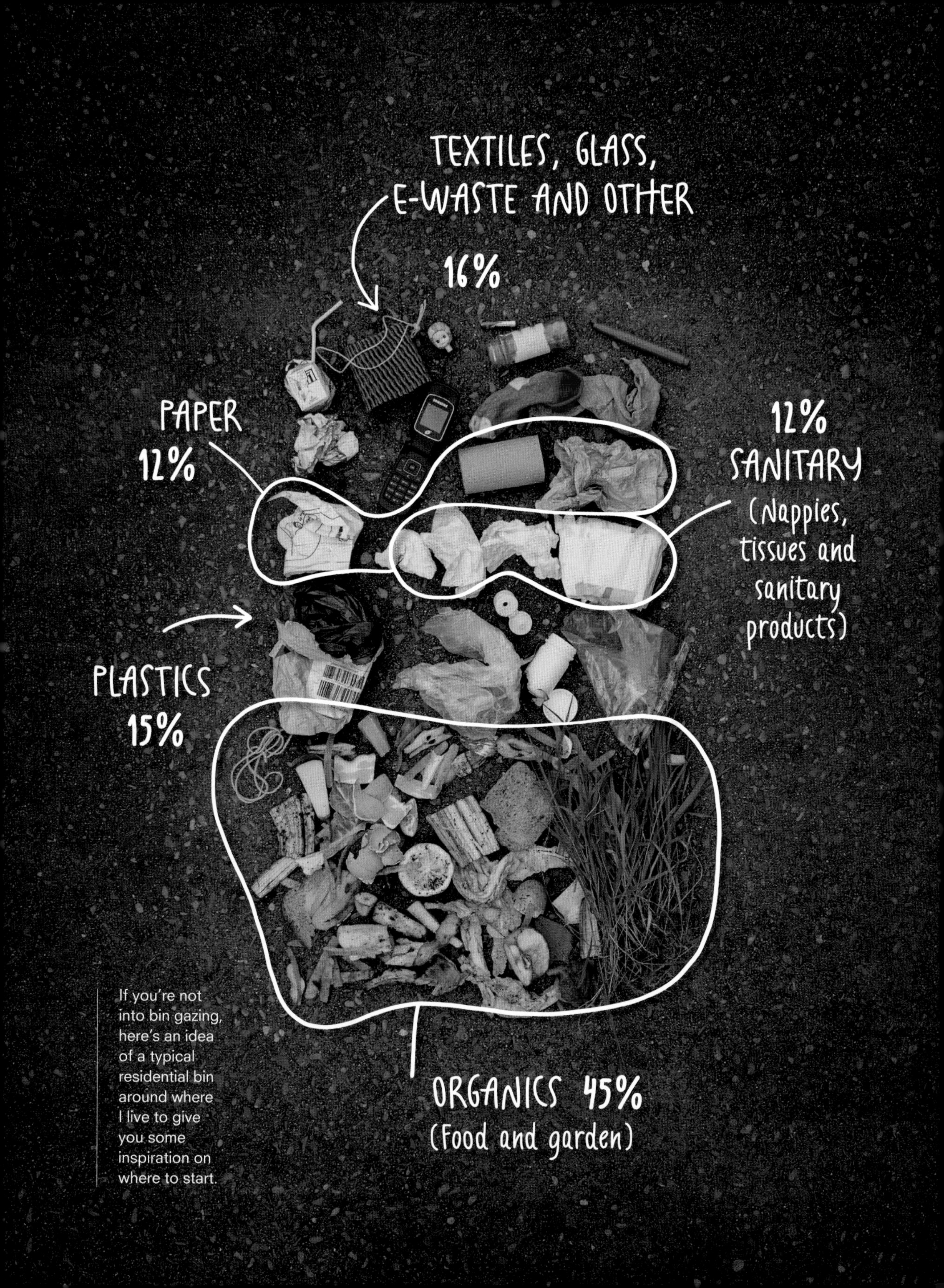

TEXTILES, GLASS,
E-WASTE AND OTHER
16%

PAPER
12%

12%
SANITARY
(Nappies,
tissues and
sanitary
products)

PLASTICS
15%

If you're not
into bin gazing,
here's an idea
of a typical
residential bin
around where
I live to give
you some
inspiration on
where to start.

ORGANICS 45%
(Food and garden)

Getting set up

Reusable bags, cups, safety razors … there is no shortage of Instagram-worthy tools to take you on a waste-reduction journey but, before you rush to the shop, there are a couple of things to think about.

1. Use what you have

I'm a sucker for a well-designed stainless steel container or good-looking reusable coffee cup. But there's a certain irony in going out and buying new shiny stuff to reduce my waste. Most of the time, I already have things I can use or, often, I find that I can get by without it.

If there's something I truly need or legit love, and I know that having it is going to help me to make a change – then, absolutely, I'll get it. But my first 'go to' is using what I have – it already exists, so let's not waste it.

I'd love to replace all of my kitchen containers with glass and stainless steel – but I've got a drawer full of plastic containers that still have a heap of life in them.

> ⊘ **TIME HACK** Using what you have means you don't have to leave the house to buy anything.

2. Over and over again

Even though reusables are where it's at, there's a slight catch. You need to *actually* reuse them, over and over again. Buying tote bags, cloth nappies or stainless steel drink bottles, then stashing them in a cupboard doesn't somehow mystically reduce your impact. Use them, or pass them on to someone who will.

> ⊘ **TIME HACK** Do what makes it easier for you to use your reusables. Have folding bags and collapsible containers that fit in your handbag, keep extra bags and cups in your car, stash old plastic bags in your glove box – whatever it takes for you to get your hands on your reusables when you need them.

Jar + rubberbands = reusable cup

This is my friend Laura's cup – so simple but so damn effective. You can even share the reusable love by making a few extras and getting amongst the awesome 'Koha Cup' movement. Check out www.uyo.co.nz for the down-low.

Making choices

Whether it's packaging or products, I get that navigating all the options and trying to make a better choice can be a bit full on. Here are a few guidelines I use when making decisions. Remember: it's not about the perfect choice, it's about better choices – rolling with any of these will mean you're making a conscious decision.

Can I take my own?

Wherever I can, I take my own bags and containers to avoid packaging. From fruit and vegies to meat, honey and takeaways, it's becoming more and more common to rock up with your own reusables to skip disposable packaging waste.

I've been known to come home with my handbag full of loose mandarins and carrots when I've forgotten my reusable bags.

Can it be reused?

Glass jars are a favourite in our house; I reuse them for storing and freezing all sorts of things. Just to complicate things, glass is heavier to transport around, so best if it's a local product or you're sure you'll reuse it.

What happens at the end of its useful life?

I choose paper over plastic because, after reusing it as much as possible, it can go into my worm farm or compost. Yep, paper also has an impact – but I prefer it over plastic, because I can compost it and return it to the earth.

How easy is it to recycle?

I choose items sold in tin cans (try to find cans with BPA-free plastic lining) and glass over plastic, as there's more demand for these in the recycling chain. Recycling glass and cans is also way more energy efficient than creating it from virgin materials.

When it comes to plastics, ♻#1 and ♻#2 normally have the most value and clear tends to have more value than coloured. Make sure you know what can be recycled in your area.

Check your local council's website to find out what gets collected and recycled where you live.

Can it be composted?

Compostable packaging and products are a good choice if they're actually going to make it to the compost – if there is a commercial collection in your area or if it states it's home compostable and that's where you're going to put it, then all good.

Can I buy less of it?

I'll always start with a micropause to check if I really need something, or if I can simplify how many different things I'm buying. If I decide to buy something, I'll see if there's a way I can reduce the packaging waste. I'll choose bulk package sizes to reduce overall waste.

Most of my pantry storage is reused tomato passata jars. See page 78 for a pic of the pantry. And yes, I always look this happy when I'm refilling my jars!

Buying in bulk doesn't have to mean buying things by the pallet load, it's as simple as buying a larger package size or switching to toilet paper in double-length rolls. This halves your plastic, and adds bonus points for changing the roll half as often.

Buying items in concentrated or solid bar form also reduces the need for excess packaging because you're getting the product without all the water (often listed as 'aqua' in the ingredients to make it sound fancy).

| ⊘ **TIME HACK** Buying in bulk should save you time and money.

Just watch out for 'theory of abundance' – when we have a lot of something we tend to use more. I've found it an issue with bulk buying chocolate.

Has it already been recycled?

Choosing products made out of recycled materials is a great way to help create demand in the recycling chain.

How does it come packaged to the store?

I do love the self-righteous feeling of going to a bulk food store and walking out with my eclectic array of refilled containers, but I also like understanding how it arrives packaged to the store. While I might be walking out package-free, if there's packaging in the supply chain, I like to be aware of it. I want to see if there's any way I can reduce it, or maybe I can take it home to reuse it.

NIC'S TAKE: ZERO WASTE

If you scroll the socials, it won't take you long before you spot an image of someone holding their year's worth of waste in a mason jar, proclaiming #zerowaste. 'Zero waste' is a term that's been trending and getting lots of attention recently. I love the fact that it's helped to push waste and sustainability into the mainstream.

The zero-waste movement aims to be aspirational, not an end point. It's a philosophy to help us get better at creating less waste, even if we can't reach 'zero'. As Anne Marie Bonneau expressed it, it's all about lots of people doing it 'imperfectly'.

The flipside is that some people get turned off by it being too extreme or appearing unattainable. One person, one year, one jar of rubbish – this can seem completely overwhelming and a bit disheartening.

If you're in the former camp and find it motivational, then get amongst it. But if it doesn't spin your wheels, then just embrace the ethos of 'less' waste.

GETTING STARTED In the following chapters, you'll find the areas in my life where I've made the biggest changes when it comes to reducing how much waste we're creating as a family. Let's get started.

EAT

> '*Tell me what you eat and*
> *I will tell you what you are.*'
> **– ANTHELME BRILLAT-SAVARIN**

Food plays a massive role in our lives. Obviously, there's the whole 'needing food to live' thing, but there's also the social and cultural sides to it, the health, self-expression, creativity, social connection – you get the picture. Food is a huge part of who we are, what we do and how we live.

The way we eat is a big deal when it comes to our own wellbeing and the wellbeing of the planet.

MY FOOD PHILOSOPHY I want to feed my family good, nourishing food in the shortest amount of time possible, while also being mindful of the impact. Food is a super-important part of our lives, but it's not my preferred hobby. I want to do what's right, but I don't want it to take over my life.

If you're a passionate foodie who spends your weekends poring over recipe books and food porn – even better. You'll still find the things I talk about relevant, but you'll be way more patient and enthusiastic about spending time in the kitchen.

A few years ago, my New Year's resolution was to go food shopping once every six weeks. My main motivation was to save time and reduce my packaging waste, but I also suspected that I would save money and we'd eat better. I diligently spread-sheeted the results (you're welcome), and they were good. Like, really good.

It took me a while to get to six weeks. Aiming to halve the number of times you go food shopping is a huge win.

In the first year of shopping this way, I saved more than NZ$4,000, reduced our packaging waste by 90%, and we ate more real food. But the best bit was that I saved nearly two working weeks of time! Yep, two whole weeks – just by going shopping less. Boom!

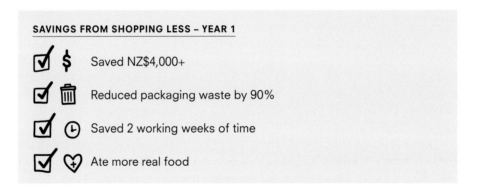

SAVINGS FROM SHOPPING LESS – YEAR 1

☑ $ Saved NZ$4,000+

☑ 🗑 Reduced packaging waste by 90%

☑ 🕐 Saved 2 working weeks of time

☑ ♥ Ate more real food

It's become my thing to prove that living more sustainably doesn't have to take more time and money – but even I was pretty surprised at how massive this change was.

Two years on and I'm still shopping this way – why wouldn't I be?

Before you panic … no, I don't spend all day in the kitchen, have an amazing garden, a house cow or feed my family only kale.

⊙ **TIME HACK** Try halving the amount of food shopping trips you do – you'll save heaps of time and cash.

Skip every second shop you would usually do.

What are we eating?

Get real

I'm going to be straight up with you. Eating more real food is a fundamental part of this journey. Processed foods are those that are manufactured and come in packets – eating less processed food is not only better for the planet but, bonus points, it's also better for us.

I'm not implying that we have to get all evangelical and become committed paleo or keto converts – I'm just talking about choosing real over processed most of the time.

> ⊘ **TIME HACK** Focusing on real food means you simplify the range of 'products' you need to shop for and keep organised.

I still eat love eating chips straight from the packet – I just don't do it as often as I used to.

Organic 'locavores'

Our way of eating relies heavily on good fresh food with seasonal variety. I'm not a complex cook – I like to let the food do the talking. I'd rather spend my money on a really good-tasting carrot than a cheap, flavourless carrot and a bottle of sauce to make it taste good. My utopia is to eat only fresh, organic, package-free, locally sourced food. My romantic vision is of a daily morning stroll through the village market, filling my basket with dewy produce and still-warm eggs. But then I remember that I have a day job, a budget and that baskets get really heavy *(and warm eggs kinda weird me out)*, so I make the best realistic choices I can.

Food miles

The less distance travelled the better, from both a nutritional and carbon perspective. I still buy bananas, despite them not growing anywhere near where I live – I just choose the fair trade ones to make them a better choice.

Local and seasonal

Eating locally also means that, by default, you're more likely to be eating food in season, which usually means fewer resources are used to grow things and it normally tastes way better.

Organic or spray free

We're only just starting to understand the impact that synthetic pesticides and fertilisers are having, not just on our own health but the health of our soil. Going for organic or spray free wherever I can means that I'm feeding my family fewer synthetic chemicals and I also feel good creating more demand for alternatives.

Ideally, I try to source from producers using regenerative farming practices – an approach that works with nature to rehabilitate and enrich a farm's entire ecosystem.

@ **FIND IT ONLINE** Check out the 'Dirty Dozen' and 'Clean 15' guides at ewg.org for help prioritising which switches to make with organic and spray-free produce.

Yep, these are cable ties holding my basket on. I use them for everything.

Sometimes I forget my reusable bag, so I just stuff items into my handbag.

How is it packaged?

We buy with our eyes. Food packaging is carefully designed and curated to tempt us, by making things look delicious and convenient.

Packaging also needs to make food items last. Supermarkets are often stocking tens of thousands of different products, which come from all over the country and the world. Food needs to be packaged so it can be transported and will last. Managing large supply chains and influencing us, as consumers, to buy it all is a hell of a juggle – things are changing but what happens to the packaging at the end of its useful life can be a long way down a company's list of priorities.

Food packaging is a big beast to tackle when it comes to reducing waste, but here are some simple packaging switches I make to lighten my impact.

1. More real food

Most real food, such as fruit and vegies, doesn't need additional packaging. It's also easy to skip those flimsy produce bags by using your own or letting them roam free.

2. Bulk up

Upsizing your packet size helps to reduce packaging. Simple switches include buying the largest bottle of milk or choosing a big bags of chips (and using containers for kids' lunches instead of those tiny multipacks with 3.2 chips).

3. BYO

Taking your own reusable bags for everything means you skip the disposable bags in the produce, bakery and bulk bin sections. A number of supermarkets are now allowing customers to use their own containers at the deli, meat and seafood counters. Bulk food, butcher and sushi shops are also great places to bring your own containers.

> ⊙ **TIME HACK** You don't even need to change where you shop
> to get amongst using your own bags and containers.

4. Alternative materials

Instead of defaulting to the product you normally buy, with packaging that ends up in the bin, look at what's next to it on the shelf. Is there another option that's:

* made from recycled materials?
* in a glass jar that can be reused?
* made of cardboard that can be composted?
* in a tin can that can be easily recycled?

If I need to go for plastics, I'll go for clear ♻#1 and ♻#2 as there's currently a better local recycling market.

Making the most of things

I remember when taco shells first hit the supermarket in the 1980s. They were so exotic and, man, did we think we were fancy eating them with mince, grated cheese and iceberg lettuce. Now, I find myself getting frustrated if I can't get avocados all year round.

These days, we can have pretty much any food imaginable and we can shoot to the shop to grab it almost any time. Choice can feel like a good thing, but it can also be time-consuming, costly and a bit overwhelming.

A game-changer for me has been just making a simple shift in my mindset. Instead of starting from the point of 'What do I feel like?' I start from 'What have I got?'. It's not about going without and eating random canned goods from your emergency kit – it's about getting creative with what you have.

If I'm stuck, I'll do a search on my phone for 'What can I make with [insert what ingredients I have]'. The World Wide Web always provides.

If I run out of an ingredient, instead of my default being to go to the shop for more, my starting point is to figure out a way to substitute something else for it.

> ⊘ **TIME HACK** Making do with what you have means you'll go to the shops less, save money and get better at using things up.

GETTING IT DONE

Food prep

We've been marketed this concept of 'convenience', that buying pre-packaged goods will save us time – that a plastic bag of pre-cut pumpkin will make life's crazy juggle just that little bit easier. I'm the first to admit that, sometimes, in some ways, it will.

But sometimes, it won't.

We've let ourselves get a bit confused by all that 'convenience' these days. We can buy pretty much anything we want, at any time of the day.

Instead of making our lives more convenient, sometimes, it means we're spending more of our time shopping.

One day, I was in the middle of making a bacon-and-egg pie and realised I'd run out of those handy frozen pastry sheets. No worries – I'll just jump in the car and drive the 4 minutes each way to my local supermarket. … it felt so easy.

But then, I took that micropause.

I could make some pastry, but that would surely take ages (and I don't like baking). It would be way quicker to shoot to the supermarket.

Or would it?

So, I did what anyone else would do – I did both.

Here's what happened.

BUYING VS. MAKING TEST

Supermarket mission results
Time taken: 28 minutes

Make-my-own pastry results
Time taken: 16 minutes

We had a very unexpected winner!

The supermarket is only a 4-minute drive from my place, and they have handy pastry in pre-rolled sheets. It feels so convenient!

But, by the time I get out of my trackies, load my kids into the car, drive, park, walk, negotiate with kids, find pastry, buy eight other things I didn't realise I needed, check out, spend $160, find car, drive home, remove children from car, unpack, get back into trackies …

You get the idea.

Making my own pastry had never entered my head. (I hate baking, remember?)

I saved a heap of time, saved money and created no extra packaging waste. I also knew and understood all of the ingredients in my pastry.

Of course, sometimes, shooting to the shop is going to be more convenient - but it's worth asking yourself the question.

Here's what I do to make food convenient without going to the shops.

Making from scratch
Before you tune out, let me explain …

I do everything I can to make the time I spend in the kitchen as efficient as possible. Along with cooking meals, I do make a few things myself – either because it's way cheaper or I haven't found a good waste-free alternative. I normally allow myself 45–60 minutes in the kitchen on a Sunday evening to make something – unless I can't be bothered, and then I don't.

⊘ **TIME HACK** Even making stuff from scratch, I'm still way better off timewise compared with going to the supermarket once (or multiple times) per week.

Have a plan
I make a loose weekly meal plan. I say 'loose' because, sometimes, I forget and, sometimes, I don't follow it, because life happens and things change. When I do, I always appreciate that I don't have to deal with the decision fatigue of deciding what to make every night. It also means that I have a plan to use all the fresh food that needs to be eaten that week.

I have a repertoire of dishes that I make regularly, and I'll meal plan based on these and what I have. Yep, I meal plan based on what I already have, not the other way around. Eating seasonally helps when it comes to adding variety to what we're eating.

I draw my meal plan on the window using a chalk marker. See page 48.

MON	LASAGNE
TUE	WRAPS
WED	SAUSAGES
THUR	PIZZA
FRI	CURRY

NIC'S TAKE: WEEKLY MEAL KIT DELIVERY

If you're into weekly meal kits, and they mean you're feeding your family healthy and nutritious real food meals, and minimising food waste by only receiving what you need, then I reckon that's awesome. If your deliveries arrive with heaps of unnecessary packaging, then have a conversation with the supplier to find out if they have any plans to change. (Don't be a jerk about it though.)

Suppliers are cropping up all the time with different offerings, including vegan, organic, local and package-free – so check out the available options in your area.

I'm also trying to convince a friend's teenager to do my baking for me – it gives her some pocket money, fills my freezer with baking and is still cheaper than buying it.

Batch cooking

Whenever I'm cooking dinner, I make as much as I possibly can. Dinner is always lunch the next day, and any leftovers are afternoon tea or put in the freezer for another time.

I did go through a stage of spending a day or two of the school holidays prepping meals, which worked well, but I now prefer just rolling it into my regular evening cooking because it doesn't feel like any more work.

Big-batch baking

I also apply my batch cooking approach to baking. If I'm making a cake or muffins, I'll cook at least double the recipe and throw a batch in the freezer. For cakes, I normally pre-cut them so I can easily grab pieces from the freezer to put in lunchboxes.

> ⏱ **TIME HACK** I sneak avocado, zucchini and sweet potato into recipes whenever I can (get those vegies in!). Putting vegies into baking and cooking is a massive time win for me; if I'm in a hurry I can just serve and go without further prep and it cuts down on the 'eat your vegetable' negotiations.

ONE BATCH
Effort = 90%   VS.   FOUR BATCHES
Effort = 100%

Recipe: All-in-one mince

I include heaps of vegies in this dish, so I can just serve and go. Typically, I'll quadruple this recipe because it's what I can fit into my two big pots. A single recipe makes enough for dinner and lunch for our family of four.

YOU WILL NEED

1 heaped tablespoon of coconut oil (or preferred cooking oil)
½ large onion (diced)
750 g beef mince (or any other red meat mince such as lamb or kangaroo)
300 ml passata or 1 can (400 g) chopped tomatoes
¼ cup tomato ketchup
500 ml chicken or vegetable stock
½ cup grated zucchini (courgettes)
½ cup grated sweet potato
½ cup grated pumpkin
½ cup grated carrot
½ cup dried brown lentils
Vegetables are substituted with whatever is in season or I have on hand.

WHAT TO DO

1. Heat oil in a pan and cook onion for 2 minutes until soft.

2. Add mince and continue cooking for a further 5 minutes.

3. Add all other ingredients and mix well.

4. Simmer until lentils are cooked through and liquid has reduced down, about 40 minutes for a single batch.

5. Freeze in meal portion sizes.

NIC'S TIPS

- Use as a base for spaghetti bolognese or lasagne
- Serve with rice, topped with smashed avocado and refried beans
- Top with mashed potatoes or cover with puff pastry to make a pie
- Stuff into roasted potatoes (leave their jackets on for extra nutrients and less waste)
- Serve on toast with a poached egg
- Make a basic tomato sauce at the same time as your mince. Follow the method above, skipping the mince and lentils. Freeze the sauce in jars, ready to add to pasta, on pizza bases or as a simmer sauce for meatballs.

Pizza is a great way to use up your leftovers. This is Tuesday night's sausage.

Pizza base is 2 cups of self-raising flour plus 3/4 cup of natural yoghurt – quantities may differ because I just make it up!

Pizza sauce recipe on previous page.

Recipe: Very very rough pastry

Makes: enough pastry for base and lid for approx. three standard-sized family pies. This recipe can be multiplied once you're in the swing of things and know how much you need.

When I first started looking for a rough puff pastry recipe, I became overwhelmed reading recipes that told me to turn the dough 90 degrees and count the number of times I rolled it. I'm sure my pastry would be puffier and flakier if I did follow those instructions, but my super-rough recipe works for us. Seriously, there's so much butter in this stuff, it's never going to taste bad!

YOU WILL NEED

2½ cups flour (I use spelt because it's what I always have, but most
    recipes recommend all-purpose white flour)
½ teaspoon salt
300 g butter (ideally, cut into quarters and put in the freezer first,
    but cold straight out of the fridge will do)
160 ml cold water (ideally, throw a couple of ice cubes in it)

WHAT TO DO

1. Sift the flour and salt into a bowl. Grate the butter into the flour mixture and loosely rub together. Add water and mix with a wooden spoon until you make a rough dough.

2. Cover with a plate and put in the fridge for 15 minutes.

3. Divide into three. Roll out one portion as needed and freeze the other two wrapped in beeswax wraps (or whatever you have lying around).

NIC'S TIP Pretty much anything tastes good in pastry, but here are some of my regular dishes:

- Vegetable quiche
- Bacon and egg pie
- Cheese and relish scrolls
- Apple and cinnamon fold-over (a lazy version of a pie)

Recipe: Bliss balls
Makes: about 40 large balls

YOU WILL NEED
3 cups dates, loosely packed (I use dried and pitted dates because
     they're cheaper and easier to source in bulk)
100 g butter
1 cup water
½ cup coconut oil
2 cups chopped sweet potato, loosely packed
½ teaspoon vanilla extract
2 cups quick-cook oats
2 heaped tablespoons cocoa powder
¼ cup chia seeds
1 large or 2 small avocados

WHAT TO DO
1. Place the dates, butter, water, coconut oil and sweet potato in a large
saucepan or pot. Cover and bring to the boil, then reduce heat and
simmer with the lid on for 10 minutes. Remove lid and simmer for a further
10 minutes to reduce liquid (stirring occasionally), until the dates are soft
and sweet potato is cooked.

2. Allow to cool, add the vanilla extract, then blend mixture to a paste.
Mix in the dry ingredients, roll into balls and store in the freezer for up
to 3 months. If the mixture is too wet, add more oats.

⊘ **TIME HACK** If you can't be bothered rolling balls, press
mixture into a slice tin, cut into squares and refrigerate.

CASE STUDY: QUITE GOOD FOOD

My friend Amber has an amazing blog called *Quite Good Food*, where she shares her plant-based recipe inspiration. She's great at keeping it real with her recipes, because she's also managing the juggle of running her own business, raising two young girls and fitting in some epic travel adventures.

Recipe: Easy homemade five-seed crackers

These crackers are gluten-free, nut-free, vegan, paleo and keto – delicious and nutritious! You can store these in bulk in a sealed container.

YOU WILL NEED

1 cup sunflower seeds
¾ cup pumpkin seeds
½ cup chia seeds
½ cup sesame seeds
¼ cup linseeds (flaxseeds)
1 teaspoon salt
1½ cups water
1 tablespoon thyme (or other dried herbs)
1 teaspoon chilli flakes (optional)

WHAT TO DO

1. Preheat the oven to 170°C fan-forced, or 180°C conventional.

2. Mix all ingredients and leave for 10–15 minutes for the chia seeds to absorb the water.

3. Give everything a good stir, then split the mixture into two lined baking trays. Use a spatula to spread out the mixture thinly. The ideal thickness is about 3 mm.

Skip the paper if you have reusable non-stick baking sheets, reuse old butter wrappers or go with a natural, unbleached parchment baking paper. Compost after you've reused it as much as possible.

4. Bake for 1 hour (switching the trays around halfway through cooking time), or until golden-brown and crisp. If the crackers don't feel crisp after 1 hour, return to the oven for another 5–10 minutes.

5. Remove trays from the oven, allow crackers to cool on the trays, then use your hands to break into pieces. Store crackers in an airtight container. They last for weeks.

Recipe: Lunchbox slice
Makes: approx. 16 pieces

YOU WILL NEED
150 g butter
2 tablespoons honey (or more for the sweet tooth)
1 cup oats
½ cup flour
½ teaspoon baking powder
½ cup shredded coconut
¼ cup chia
¼ cup sesame seeds
¼ cup buckwheat groats
½ cup dried apricots or sultanas

WHAT TO DO
1. Preheat the oven to 180°C. In a saucepan over low heat, melt butter and honey. Remove from the heat and mix in the dry ingredients. Make sure there's a bit of butter pooling on top.

2. Place mixture in a 20 x 20 cm slice tin and bake for 12–15 minutes.

3. Allow to cool, cut into slices and keep in the fridge for up to a week.

NIC'S TIP For this to work, the only dry ingredients you really need are the oats, flour, baking powder and coconut … all the rest is freestyle. So, feel free to swap out ingredients for your own personal faves.

OTHER LUNCH BOX IDEAS:

- Dinner leftovers
- Hummus and crackers/vegies
- Pikelets
- Fritters
- Celery or banana with nut butter
- Eggs, eggs, eggs

- Pasta salad
- Smoothie – freeze in a reusable pouch
- Yoghurt and muesli
- Oven-baked potato or kumara chips
- Cheese on toast

- 'Lazy sushi' – roll balls of rice with something in the middle
- Mini quiche – cook egg and vegies in muffin trays

Make things in bulk and freeze, or cook extra of whatever you are making at dinner time.

Whole or
cut fruit

Wholegrain bread

Popcorn

Frozen berries
in yoghurt

Dried
fruit

Leftover pizza

Beetroot
hummus

Bliss
ball

Mixed nuts

Vegetables

Boiled eggs

Peanut butter on
banana halves

Pretzels

Avocado

Recipe: Vanilla extract

3 vanilla bean pods,
    split down the middle
300 ml vodka

1. Place vanilla pods in a clean
glass bottle (I use a 300 ml
tomato sauce bottle) and cover
with vodka.
2. Store in a dark place for at
least one month before using.

You can keep topping up with
vodka as you use it. Mine's been
going for nearly 2 years and is
only just starting to lose its flavour.

⊘ **TIME HACK** For crackers in a hurry, cut up a French baguette
into thin rounds, drizzle with oil, sprinkle with salt and bake in
the oven on a medium heat for 10 minutes each side.

Recipe: Basic crackers

YOU WILL NEED
1 cup flour
¼ cup water
½ teaspoon salt
2 tablespoons olive oil
½ cup finely grated cheese (optional)

WHAT TO DO
1. Preheat the oven to 180°C.
2. Combine all the ingredients into a bowl and form a dough. Roll out
the dough as thinly as possible – about 1 mm is ideal. (Use or borrow a
pasta maker if you're doing a bulk bake.)
3. Cut dough into the cracker size you want, place onto lightly floured
baking trays and bake for about 10 minutes.

NIC'S TIP I store these in a jar in the freezer – it keeps the crackers fresh
and also puts them out of the line of sight of my family, so they aren't all
gone within hours. It sounds mean to hide them, but I know you're with me.

NECESSITY IS THE MOTHER OF INVENTION

Given that I only go to the supermarket every six weeks, if I run out of something, I have to figure out a way to get around it that doesn't involve going to the shop. I discovered that you can find a substitute for pretty much anything.

Here are some of the substitutions I've put into action:

Original ingredients	My substitution
1 egg	1 tablespoon chia seeds
1 teaspoon baking powder	¼ teaspoon baking soda (bicarb soda) + ½ teaspoon lemon juice
1 cup breadcrumbs	1 cup rolled oats
1 cup sour cream	1 cup yoghurt + 1 tablespoon lemon juice
1 cup cream	²/₃ cup milk + ¹/₃ cup butter (not suitable for whipping, though)
1 cup oil	1 cup apple sauce (for baking)
1 cup coconut milk	1 cup desiccated coconut + 1 cup water, blended and strained
1 cup tomato sauce	¹/₃ cup tomato paste + ²/₃ cup water + salt/sugar to taste (most tomato forms can be substituted for one another)

One of my favourite discoveries came about when I ran out of vanilla extract. You can make your own, simply by putting vanilla pods in vodka! Granted, it takes a month to steep (→ see recipe, opposite), so I ended up being very old-fashioned and borrowing some vanilla from my neighbour, but I'll never need to buy those tiny little bottles again.

Fresh produce

Gardening is the panacea of sustainability – from organic garden to plate with no food miles. If you're into gardening – embrace it! The more people who are growing their own food, the better for everyone.

But here's the thing … I'm an average-to-poor gardener, and that's being generous. I'm getting better, but I don't love it enough to spend all my spare time gardening. I'm hoping my love for it will develop with age but, in the meantime, I'm happy with growing a few basics, then doing what I can to make better choices in other ways.

I love that gardening helps my kids understand where food comes from and keeps us grounded in the downright miracle that is Mother Nature.

WHAT WE GROW

I pick things that are super easy to grow and give me a big return.

COS LETTUCE Grows all year round, keeps on giving, doesn't need full sun, grows in anything. Harvest the outside leaves first.

NZ SPINACH Self-sows, use it in smoothies, replaces salad greens for at least 6 months of the year. Looks fancy as a garnish.

CHERRY TOMATOES Grows easily in summer, kids can self-serve.

LEBANESE CUCUMBERS Low maintenance, also in the kids' garden drive-through.

ZUCCHINIS (COURGETTES) Blink and they grow. Grate and freeze in muffin tins for when they're $15 a kilo in winter.

NIC'S GARDEN HACKS

SHARE THE LOAD Talk to friends and neighbours, and grow different things so you can swap – you'll double your range, just like that!

SHARING SHED We take our excess produce to a sharing shed at my daughter's school and take home other produce in exchange. (Community gardens and crop swaps are also great, and check out food-sharing apps such as Olio.)

DON'T STRESS If gardening is really not your thing, it's all good! Find someone who's into it and keen to share their excess produce – make them dinner in exchange.

START WITH ONE THING It's amazing what you can grow in a pot on the windowsill, and, who knows, it may spark a passion you never knew you had.

Be super careful if foraging mushrooms, though – some mushrooms are poisonous. Find someone experienced to take you and show you the ropes.

GET FORAGING Lots of great produce is just hanging around your neighbourhood, either growing in the wild, or planted by councils or good people wanting to share. @ **FIND IT ONLINE** Check out fallingfruit.org, or arm yourself with a book from Pat Collins (AU) or Julia Sich's (NZ).

Kitchen window - we can
easily see what is growing
and it's quickly accessible
while we are cooking.

OUR WINTER GARDEN

Cabbages from
Mike's sauerkraut
adventure

Companion plant
for pest control

NZ spinach

CASE STUDY: FAMILY GARDEN CO-OP

When it comes to gardening, the Moore and Lind families have combined their powers. The Moores had the space, the Linds had the know-how, and working together saves them time and creates some accountability. With eight kids between them, eating fresh, organic produce is now way more affordable and it's an awesome way for the kids to learn about where their food comes from and about working together.

Kath, Mel and some of their crew

Buying produce

Weekly delivery

Every Friday morning, a box of produce (and eggs) arrives via subscription on our doorstep. There are a heap of different options and companies to choose from – I go for one that is predominantly local, seasonal and spray free. The delivery comes packed in a cardboard box, which I leave out the following week for collection and reuse.

I could ride my bike down to the farmers' market every weekend with my reusable produce bags and have the same result – sometimes I do, and I love it. But I get a delivery (a lot of farmers' markets also deliver) because I like to save time, and I know that, sometimes, getting to the farmers' market isn't going to happen because we're away, or I'm too busy, or it's too cold.

Roadside stalls

I'm a big fan of buying things from roadside stalls – it's as local and seasonal as it gets. It's cheap (or sometimes free) and it saves produce from going to waste in people's backyards.

If produce is already packed in plastic bags, I'll take it out and leave the bag behind to be reused.

Shared produce

When I'm offered produce out of people's gardens, I always say 'yes' and figure out what to do with it when I get home. My default is normally grating and freezing it in muffin tins or ice cube trays. I then store it free-flow in bags or containers, to add to cooking or throw into my morning smoothie.

Seriously, there's not much you can't freeze.

I'm constantly amazed at freezers ... they suspend food in time, how cool is that?!?

FREEZE IT ALL, BABY

AVOCADOS Scoop out, freeze flesh on an oven tray and then store in an airtight container in the freezer (*my best freezer victory this season*).

LIMES/LEMONS Cut into wedges, freeze on a tray and store in the freezer, ready for summer drinks (*ice, garnish and flavour all in one!*).

GREEN BEANS Cut to the length you like to cook with, then blanch in boiling water for 2 minutes. Once cool and dry, freeze on an oven tray then store in a bag or container. (*I actually skip the blanching step, because I can't be bothered, but it does retain the colour and texture better.*)

ZUCCHINI (COURGETTE) AND PUMPKIN Remove skin from pumpkin, grate, squeeze out excess liquid and pack into muffin tins or ice cube trays to freeze. Once frozen, transfer to a bag or container and store in the freezer. (*Great for adding to baking, mince dishes and omelettes.*)

CASE STUDY: VEGAN RECIPE FOR NON-VEGANS

Ange is a mum of two who is the powerhouse behind Ripe Deli, an Auckland institution. Ripe is all about bringing people local, seasonal and nutritious food. As if the awesome food isn't enough, I love the fact that Ange is driven to do things as sustainably as possible, from minimising food waste in all her kitchens and encouraging customers to use reusable containers, to having one of the largest worm farms in Auckland.

I asked Ange to share one of her favourite easy vegan recipes. I can confirm it's a bloody great one to serve to meat eaters like my husband. It's also an awesome recipe to use up all those random vegies left in the fridge at the end of the week.

Recipe: Mexican black bean and vegetable stew

Another great option to batch cook and throw in the freezer

YOU WILL NEED

400 g can black or kidney beans
500 g butternut pumpkin or kumara,
     diced into small (3 cm) cubes
1 tablespoon olive oil
1 teaspoon sea salt
1 onion, peeled and finely diced
3 garlic cloves, crushed and finely
     chopped
2 teaspoons smoked paprika
2 teaspoons ground cumin
2 teaspoons ground coriander
1–2 teaspoons chilli flakes (*less
     if you don't like it spicy*)
2 cups diced vegetables (e.g.,
     zucchini/courgette, eggplant,
     capsicum, mushrooms, celery,
     leek, spinach, carrot – whatever
     you want to use up)
1 teaspoon fresh oregano or
     ½ teaspoon dried oregano
1 cup vegetable stock
2 x 400 g cans crushed tomatoes
1 cup frozen corn

WHAT TO DO

1. Preheat the oven to 180°C. Lightly grease a baking tray with olive oil. Drain and rinse the beans.

2. In a mixing bowl, toss the diced pumpkin or kumara in the olive oil and salt. Place mixture on the prepared baking tray and bake for 10 minutes, or until just cooked through.

3. Remove from the oven and set aside.

4. In a large saucepan over a medium heat, add a dash of oil and fry the onion, garlic and spices for a few minutes. Add additional chopped vegetables and cook for a further 3–5 minutes.

5. Add the oregano, stock, tomatoes, corn, beans and roasted pumpkin or kumara. Cook over a medium heat for 20 minutes.

6. Season to taste with salt and freshly ground black pepper, then serve.

This is Ange.

The fridge

Meat

Hi – my name is Nic, and I'm a reducetarian. I'm actually really into this as a general philosophy for life (it's not going without, it's about everything in moderation), but let's talk about it in terms of meat.

Veganism and vegetarianism are often held up as the mantles of sustainable living – and to those of you that do it, I salute you, I really do. But, as with most things in life, the debate over meat consumption is complex and very emotional. Eating meat isn't going away any time soon, and I reckon there's a lot to be said for finding better ways of doing it. Here's how I roll.

1. We eat less meat

This is where the reducetarianism bit comes in.

My husband used to eat steak for breakfast so, to be fair, we had some easy wins to get us started.
- I aim for one meat-free day a week.
- I make meat go further with smaller cuts and adding more plant-based ingredients (my mince dishes are now only about 40% mince!).
- When I eat out, I order the meat-free option – it's a way of getting more adventurous with what I eat and finding inspiration for cooking.

2. I buy better

I shop at my local butcher because they handle everything from farming and processing to curing and selling. They're big on regenerative farming practices and animal welfare, and use few synthetic chemicals. They're good humans doing good things, and I feel stoked to be able to support them.

Their meat is better quality, but it's more expensive. By eating less and buying in bulk, however, I'm still better off – problem solved.

3. I buy in bulk

I buy in quarter- or half-beast amounts – I do this to save time and money. Half a beast will last us nearly 12 months – I won't buy any more until we've used up everything we have. I also buy chickens in bulk, and freeze them whole in a container.

I only freeze chicken in containers that can be washed properly in hot soapy water between use.

4. I skip the packaging

In the morning of the day I pick up my meat order, I drop off a bunch of large empty containers and the butcher will put the unpackaged fresh meat straight into them. I pick these up in the afternoon and take them home to pack it down.

I use whatever I have on hand to freeze the meat in meal portion sizes – plastic ice cream and yoghurt containers (my mum normally has a stash of containers in her recycling bin), heavy-duty plastic bags that my bulk dry food comes in, and glass jars for bacon. There's all sorts of fancy silicone wraps and reusable storage bags you can buy to freeze things in, but I'm a big fan of reusing what you have. Whatever you use for food storage, just make sure it's clean and hygienic.

A friend has made me some reusable freezer bags out of food-grade PUL waterproof fabric that I'm currently trialling. If they work, I could give these to the butcher for them to pack straight into – saves me a bit more time.

Meat and dairy scraps go here. See page 89.

Pumpkin from a friend's garden

STRAWBERRY JAM

COCONUT VEG

Made in Mrs Pickle's kitchen

BOKASHI
do not eat me ☺

Yoghurt made in a glass jar. See page 74.

BROWN RICE MALT SYRUP

Cheese in beeswax wrap

Damp cloth to keep greens fresh

Reusable produce bags are great for storage.

KET

Maple Syrup

soda SOURCE

⊘ **TIME HACK** Take your containers with you to the supermarket whenever you're buying fresh or deli meat over the counter. Or try taking them to the butcher and stock up your freezer with bulk pet food.

Dairy

When I first started making changes, I found that dairy was a bit of a mission but, now, more and more companies are starting to offer good alternatives, and it feels like it's only going to get better.

Milk

I buy in glass and refill my bottles. To save me having to go every week, I also sometimes take my large containers to a milk vending machine *(it's a Kiwi thing – you Aussies should get on board)*, buy in bulk and freeze it in glass bottles. Some dairy farms in New Zealand offer vending machines with both raw and pasteurised milk, and refillable glass bottle options are cropping up all the time.

A lot of these vending machines are automatic – you enter in the volume of milk you want, insert cash or card to pay, and it dispenses the amount of milk you have selected into your own bottles *(it's just you and the machine, so no need to feel awkward)*.

At some farmers' markets, you'll find old-fashioned vats with a tap on the side, which the operator will use to fill your bottles and charge you by volume.

If freezing, just leave a decent air gap at the top of the bottle.

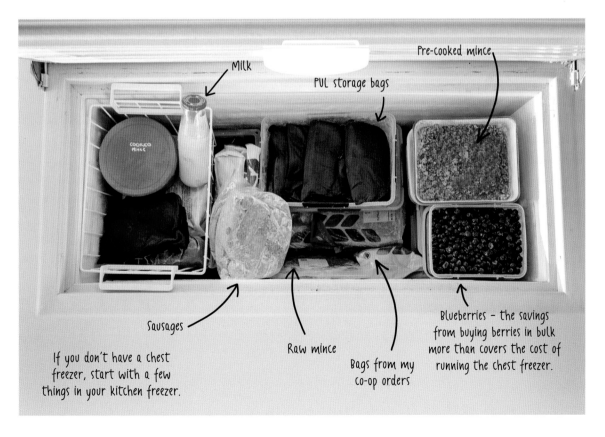

Milk

PUL storage bags

Pre-cooked mince

Sausages

If you don't have a chest freezer, start with a few things in your kitchen freezer.

Raw mince

Bags from my co-op orders

Blueberries – the savings from buying berries in bulk more than covers the cost of running the chest freezer.

⊘ **TIME HACK** You can even get a group going, where everyone takes a turn to do the milk run each week.

If you're lucky, you might live somewhere where you can get glass bottles delivered and they'll accept your empties the following week. *Yup, the way it used to be.*

If glass doesn't work for you, buying milk in the largest plastic bottle you can is also better than buying lots of smaller bottles.

Cheese

It's easy to find unpackaged specialty cheese at markets and deli counters. However, as much as I love my children, I can't justify spending $45 a kilo on something that may or may not be swimming around in a lunchbox bath of yoghurt and squashed raisins at the end of the day. To buy in bulk, I take my own containers to the supermarket counter and buy a basic cheddar. Even though it comes to them in a 20 kg block wrapped in a layer of plastic, it still means less plastic overall. I wrap the cheese in beeswax wraps and then store in an airtight container in the fridge.

→ You can freeze cheese, but it does make the texture a bit crumblier.

But I'm still searching for a better option – one that is local, package-free and affordable. I don't ask for much, do I?

Several people have suggested I try making my own. I laughed. A lot. I have absolute respect for the art of cheese-making, and I'm acutely aware that my attention span wouldn't be compatible.

Butter

I buy several blocks at once from the supermarket. I go for butter in plain wrappers that can be reused as baking paper then composted (if you're not sure what it's made of, email the supplier and double-check it's compostable).

I make yoghurt in a glass jar because exposing plastics to high temperatures can cause potentially harmful chemicals to leach out – and I swear it also tastes better out of glass. ↘

Yoghurt

Pretty much the whole internet told me how easy it was to make my own yoghurt. I tried six batches and none of them worked – I think I was too lax measuring the temperature. Every batch had a weird consistency and my family just wasn't into it. Currently, I buy the supermarket sachets and make them in my home yoghurt maker. And I've managed to nail making coconut yoghurt (→ see page 76).

The last thing I want to do is put you off making your own yoghurt. It's a really great option, and lots of people are nailing it. But … I also want to reiterate the fact that, sometimes, things don't work for you and it's okay to give yourself a break. I'll take another run at making my own yoghurt again but, for now, I'm just letting it go.

Not dairy

If you're a nut mylk kinda person, I highly recommend making your own – it tastes SO much better (and those tetra packs are a bit of a mission to recycle). Tetra packs are mixed materials – they're a combo of paper, plastic and foil – which makes them niggly to recycle and means there's very little value in them.

Bliss balls

Leftover fruit

Vegies for smoothies and stock

Reused jars - write on top for easy identification.

Recipe: Coconut yoghurt

YOU WILL NEED

1 x 300–400 g can coconut cream (it needs to be the good stuff – no added thickeners, fillers or emulsifiers)

2 tablespoons coconut yoghurt (good-quality store-bought or from a previous homemade batch), or 2 probiotic capsules, or ½ teaspoon probiotic powder

WHAT TO DO

1. Heat the coconut cream in a saucepan to approx 40°C. Pour into a clean jar.

2. Add coconut yoghurt or open the probiotic capsules and sprinkle the powder. Secure the lid, shake gently and put in a warm place (at least 20°C) – a kitchen shelf will normally work, and other options include a hot-water cupboard, a yoghurt maker with warm water, in a closed oven with the light on for a bit of warmth. Leave for 24–48 hours.

3. Put in the fridge (where it will further thicken).

Recipe: Almond mylk

YOU WILL NEED

1 cup almonds

1 litre water (filtered, ideally)

1 teaspoon maple syrup (optional)

WHAT TO DO

1. Put almonds in bowl and cover with water. Allow to soak for about 12 hours.

2. Drain almonds and rinse a couple of times. Place the drained almonds in a blender. Add water and maple syrup and blend until smooth.

3. Strain mixture through a piece of muslin or cheese cloth. Blow your mind by how much better tasting it is than store-bought.

⊘ **TIME HACK** Find a friend or two who are also into almond mylk and take turns at making it. For a super-quick non-strained version, blend 4 tablespoons almond butter with 1 litre water (and optional maple syrup).

NIC'S TIP I add the leftover pulp to porridge, smoothies, soups, stews, baking – you name it, a bit of nut roughage is always good. If you're not going to use it straight away, throw it in the freezer.

Cashew milk is also a winner – just swap the almonds for cashews, and you can even skip the straining.

The pantry

Buying pantry staples in bulk is like hitting the trifecta – it saves you time, money and packaging waste. Winning can be as simple as buying things at the supermarket in the largest packet size you can (one big bag of rice will have a lot less packaging than 20 small bags), through to buying in wholesale quantities direct from the supplier.

The co-op

I belong to an organic buying co-operative. This is a group of people who get together to have enough purchasing power to buy directly from the supplier. Buying in bulk this way means cheaper prices (yay, affordable organics!) and less packaging waste. A co-op can work for any type of product, but the one I belong to is for pantry ingredients – think nuts, seeds, flours, grains, oils and canned goods.

> @ **FIND IT ONLINE** New Zealanders: to find a co-op in your area, check out Aotearoa Food Co-op Community on Facebook.
> Australians: just do an internet search – they're everywhere!

Each co-op runs slightly differently, but this is what happens with mine. Once every three months, from the comfort of my couch, I fill in a spreadsheet with what I need – I can buy in bulk quantities or, in the spirit of a co-op, I can share these bulk quantities with other people. When the goods arrive, I take my bags there, have a chat and weigh out what I need. And I'm done.

I don't order everything every three months, because I run out of stuff at different times.

Co-op shopping list. Here's my most recent order:

2.5 kg almonds	1 kg popping corn
2 kg cashews	5 kg rolled oats
6 x cans coconut cream	20 kg spelt flour
3 kg dried apricots	2 kg sushi rice
5 L olive oil	6 x bottles tomato passata
3.5 kg pasta	6 x bottles tomato sauce

> **AVOIDING COST BLOWOUTS** Buying in bulk means you're outlaying more money upfront. Tackling one product at a time, or putting money away at each shop, can make it way easier to afford.

Apple scrap vinegar – made from fermented cores and peels. Use in place of apple cider vinegar.

Containers bought second-hand. Try asking your local café or restaurant for their empty bulk jars.

Passata jars

Bread stays fresh longer in beeswax wraps.

Soda stream – skip the plastic soda bottles and make your own fizzy drinks.

Practice safe storage
Luckily, I've never had a problem with any pantry pests. Just make sure everything is properly sealed, and in a cool place out of the direct sun. You can also throw stuff in the freezer to help retain freshness.

If you're worried about how much space you'll need – never fear, it's really not that much! (→ To check out what my bulk storage looks like, see page 122.)

The bulk food store
For food items that I don't need in large quantities, I take my own containers to the bulk food store (or use the bulk bins at your local supermarket).

> ⊘ **TIME HACK** Start by emptying the products you already have at home into jars and containers – this will give you a feel for how much you use and get you used to the containers.

@ **FIND IT ONLINE** If you're not near a bulk store, there are online stores that use minimal packaging. Check out goodfor.co.nz and thesourcebulkfoods.com.au.

I get things such as:
• Spices
• Peanut butter (grind your own – it comes out warm, which is kind of weird)
• Cocoa (that stuff is just too messy to share in bulk quantities)
• Snacks – pretzels, lollies, trail mixes
• Balsamic vinegar

You can get so much more – even dried pet food – but I get the rest through the co-op because it saves me time. Every time I go to the bulk store, I buy enough to last me 3–4 months, time-saving and all!

The supermarket
For the stuff that I do buy at the supermarket – I think about the packaging. For each purchase, I ask myself:
• Can I get it without packaging?
• What's the largest packet size?
• Can I compost or reuse the packaging at home?
• If I do choose plastic, is it ♻#1 or ♻#2 , or made from recycled materials?

> ⊘ **TIME HACK** Every time you go to the supermarket, choose just one product to switch. Start ordering online – it's easier to order in bulk, it stops you from being tempted by things you don't need and it's easy to re-order once you've got a list going. Just have a conversation with them about using your own bags.

BUYING BULK

If you've never been to a bulk food store
before, I get that it can feel a bit awkward.
On your first trip, just choose a couple of easy
things to buy to get you started - something
like popping corn, baking soda and rice.
Here's how it works:

Weigh

When you arrive at
the store, hand over
your empty containers
to be weighed.

Label
and pay

Bring your
containers

Cloth bags, ziplock
bags, ice cream
containers, jars - use
whatever you have

Fill

Go shopping and
fill up your
containers.

Bread

Every six weeks, I head to the local bakery to stock up on bread. I take my own reused plastic bags and throw it all in the freezer.

> ⊘ **TIME HACK** You can do the same at the supermarket if they have an in-store bakery – just give them a heads up so they can get it ready for you.

Eating out

I'd love to say that my body is a temple and nothing passes my lips that hasn't been lovingly prepared in my own kitchen, using unpackaged, organic, free-range ingredients. But let's keep it real – eating out is awesome, and it's a huge part of our modern lives. The cool thing is that there are easy ways to eat out with less impact.

TAKEAWAY TAKE AWAYS

If we're getting Thai, Indian or anything else that comes in a plastic container, this is what we do:

1. Phone ahead and ask if it's okay to bring our own containers.

2. Get there 5 minutes early and hand them over. I normally take glass-bottom containers with leak-proof plastic lids, but I've also been known to take pots before - and almost got away with claiming the food was homemade.

3. Eat the food and swear aloud to everyone in earshot that it tastes better because it's not in cheap plastic.

- If we buy fish and chips, we compost the paper. Same goes for pizza – compost the box. I've considered taking an oven tray for the pizza, but still think that might be a bit weird (watch this space).
- For lunchtime sushi, take a plate from the office and use the big bottles of soy on the tables to avoid those tiny little plastic fish with their little red noses. If I'm getting a cheeky sweet treat, but don't have a container with me, I'll often just ask for it on a serviette that I'll take home and compost. I've asked for a piece of caramel slice to get put straight onto my hand before – it was the quickest way to get it into my mouth.
- When I'm going to a food truck, I just rock up with my own container and hand it over. I'm getting better at remembering to have some cutlery with me too, but if I forget – I don't beat myself up about it.
- If we go out for a restaurant meal, I try to remember to take a container with me (often a serviette will do it, unless of course it's soup). There are almost always leftovers, which I can normally bundle up and use for lunchboxes the next day.

As my friend Brent says, 'Just walk up like you own the place.' If you hand over your container with confidence, no one will even question it.

I did once go to a new café to discover they only served food in disposable packaging (it was a council regulation thing before you get all judgey like I did). I walked around the corner to the charity store and bought a plate, knife and fork for $0.60 and took them back to the café to eat my food. Then the staff at the café gave it a wash for me and I took them back to the charity store. I considered it a rental system. I get it – I went too far and no normal person is going do that, but I had the time that day and it's made for a good story.

Straws

I keep a few stainless-steel straws in my handbag for when I'm out with the kids. When I order beverages, I try to remember to ask for no straw – but I still sometimes get caught out with them popping up, unexpectedly, in drinks.

A STRAW-TASTROPHY

On a night out with friends, I ordered a round of cocktails and asked the bartender for no straws. She was really supportive and praised me for doing the right thing. I felt stoked and strolled back to our table to await our guilt-free round of drinking.

I looked up to see her walking towards us with a tray of glasses – each glass beautifully adorned with not one, but two straws. Her eyes met mine, and her hospitality smile dissolved into a look of sheer panic. She stopped in her tracks and started wildly pulling straws out of drinks.

Despite our best intentions, sometimes, we just roll on autopilot. It may take a few goes to create a new habit.

Or I'll sit down and enjoy my coffee in a proper crockery cup.

Takeaway cups

Coffee: I always make sure I've got a kickass reusable coffee cup – I need to love it, otherwise I won't want to use it.

Smoothies: Sometimes, despite everything else in a café being served in proper crockery, the smoothies arrive in a disposable cup. I now know that I should ask first. Frequently, I've had them put straight into my reusable water bottle instead.

Water bottles

I've always been pretty good at taking my reusable drink bottle with me, and now I'm good at asking to have it refilled when I'm out and about. I felt a bit awkward at first, but I've found that cafés are totally down with it. There are even apps that tell you where the nearest water fountain is (check out WeTap Drinking Fountain Finder or look for stickers from RefillNZ on café windows).

I have a friend who used to drink out of people's garden hoses when out exercising – I'll give him points for resourcefulness – but I've only just stopped to question the social appropriateness of it.

@ **FIND IT ONLINE** There are awesome websites and apps to hook you up
with cafés and businesses who are doing their bit: cogo.co and uyo.co.nz,
plus responsiblecafes.org

83

———

EAT

Booze

When we're heading out to a party, we'll normally take a bottle of vodka, a couple of
bottles of homemade soda from the Soda Stream and a bag of frozen lime wedges.

If you're into beer, get yourself a 'growler' – a reusable bottle just under 2 litres,
which lots of craft beer suppliers are offering refills for these days. Or go old-school
Kiwi with the swappa crate. For the wine crew, keep your ear out as there are bars and
vineyards that offer wine on tap.

Food waste

Food waste is a HUGE deal. In developed countries, a heap of the wastage comes from consumers after purchase. (Yep, that's you and me.) I've curated some pretty full-on stats to do the talking. I'm not doing this to overwhelm you – I just want to give you some perspective on how big this issue is. The awesome news is that reducing our food waste is actually a super-easy fix.

FOOD-WASTE STAT PARTY

- If food waste were a country, it would be the third-largest greenhouse-gas emitter, after the United States and China! – *UNenvironment.org*
- One-third of food produced globally goes to waste. – *UNenvironment.org*
- New Zealand creates enough food waste annually to feed the whole of Dunedin for nearly three years. – *Lovefoodhatewaste.co.nz*
- In Australia, one in five shopping bags end up in the bin = $3,800 worth of groceries per household each year. – *OzHarvest.org*
- Every year, 25% of all fresh water consumed and 300 million barrels of oil are used to produce food that goes to waste. – *Lovefoodhatewaste.co.nz*
- Eliminating global food waste would save 4.4 million tonnes of CO_2 per year, which is the equivalent of taking one in four cars off the road. – *OzHarvest*

Get your priorities straight

When it comes to dealing with food waste, there's a priority order that can be helpful to keep in mind:

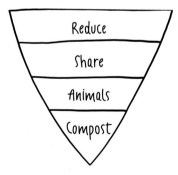

1. Reduce food waste.

2. Share excess produce with people (start with friends, neighbours, those in need, or use apps such as Olio).

3. Use excess food to feed pets and other animals (just know what they can and can't eat).

4. Compost, compost, compost (→ see page 86)

Make do, can do

Probably the biggest thing I do to reduce waste is rolling with a 'make do' mindset, and using what I have first. I'm totally aware that this is sometimes mildly frustrating for my husband. This means that I'm using things up before they have a chance to become waste. I take a certain satisfaction seeing our fridge pretty much empty at the end of each week. Here's how this works in practice:

Shop better

When I do go shopping, I check what we already have and make sure I take a list. I'm not a robot; I still get tempted by stuff I don't need – a list helps keep me on track.

Use leftovers

One night a week is leftover night. I normally make 'Pizza Surprise', where I throw anything that's left in the fridge onto a pizza. Despite all my other cooking efforts, this is still my kids' favourite meal.

Tuesday's leftover sausage

FOOD STORAGE HACKS

Storing food correctly makes it last way longer.

- Wrap leafy greens in a damp tea towel.
- Leave the pip in a halved avocado to stop it browning.
- Store carrots in an airtight container lined with an absorbent cloth.
- Put milk on the shelves as opposed to the door because it stays colder. (Who knew?)
- Keep your onions and potatoes away from each other – they really don't get on well together.
- Trim asparagus and herbs, and store them upright in some water.

Sweet potato from last night's roast

Navigate food dates

A 'best before' date is normally just an indication of quality, not safety, so I've learned to be a bit more lax. If products get close to their 'best before' date, or are getting past it, I'll throw them in the freezer until I'm ready to use them. Note that you need to stick to the 'use by' date, however, for food safety reasons.

Eat this bit!

Save it for later

In the freezer, I have a container where I add random half bananas and pieces of fruit and vegies that are bruised or haven't been eaten. I'll then use these in smoothies.

When I don't have time to prep, I've been known to throw whole zucchini in the freezer. Yeah, they go a bit mushy when defrosted, but they're still good for adding to soups and stews.

Use it all

I try to cook nose-to-tail and root-to-shoot, cooking mainly whole chickens (using the bones for stock), leaving on potato skins and using things like broccoli stalks and beetroot leaves. Any offcuts are popped in the freezer to use in soups and stocks. I save meat fat and use it for frying – mmm, fat.

And this bit too.

Composting

Unless you're prepared to do things like cooking and powdering your eggshells for the extra calcium and making enough banana skin cakes to feed the neighbourhood (yep, banana skin cakes are a thing), it's likely that you'll end up with some food waste.

Because I get carried away and like to understand how things work, I have three different systems for dealing with mine. Clearly, you don't need to go that far!

There's a whole world of information out there on how to rot things, but I've focused on what I do.

Oh, FAQ number one: composting does *not* smell.

> ⊘ **TIME HACK** If you start composting all your food waste, you won't even have to line your rubbish bin.

> @ **FIND IT ONLINE** If you want to dig deeper, check out these resources:
> https://compostcollective.org.nz or https://compostrevolution.com.au/

1. Worm farm

Worms are pretty freaken incredible creatures. Their ability to transform all sorts of 'waste' into a nutrient-dense usable product is a constant source of fascination for me.

I have a wheelie bin–style system that can cope with a lot of volume, now that it's up and running. Worms will eat most produce, but can be a bit fussy when it comes to acidic, spicy or highly processed food.

Once you've got the hang of it, they are hugely efficient and give you amazing material to use on your garden.

Here's how to get started:

- Three-quarter fill your bin with free-draining bedding material (e.g. shredded paper, compost, potting mix and dead leaves).
- Add around 500 g live worms (you need to source the right type of worm, so find someone else with a worm farm, or buy them – they can even be sent in the mail).
- Add finely chopped food scraps.
- Cover with damp newspaper.

As a super-rough guide, worms can eat about their body weight in food each day (e.g. 500 g worms = 500 g of food waste consumed). So, as the worms multiply (and man, do they!), the volume they can cope with will obviously increase.

Unless you're like my friend Liz, though, who is totally freaked out by worms. She's also terrified of ET and cows, so I feel like she's one out of the bag.

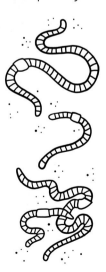

Worms like a mix of green (nitrogen rich) and brown (carbon rich) materials.

Green	Brown
Green leaves	Paper and newspaper (but not glossy)
Vegetable and fruit scraps (avoid acidic foods like citrus and onions)	Egg cartons (shredded)
	Eggshells (crushed)
	Used teabags/leaves and coffee grounds
	Dried leaves
	Hair and the contents of my vacuum cleaner (assuming you're not vacuuming up plastic)

2. Compost bin

This is a good old-fashioned black bin in the corner of our backyard, where I throw pretty much any produce that the worms don't like, as well as random stuff from the garden (to keep the green and brown balance).

> ⊘ **TIME HACK** If having your own compost is not your thing, chat to your neighbour or check out sharewaste.com and hook up with someone who has space in their bin.

3. Bokashi bin

This is a sealed bin that ferments food to a point where it's inert enough to dig into the garden or add to the compost. It's a great option if you don't have any outdoor space. I use this for all the hard-to-compost things such as meat and dairy, and the random stuff that comes home in kids' lunchboxes.

If you don't have outside space, you can keep a worm farm on a balcony or in a garage, and a bokashi bin can even live inside.

> ⊘ **TIME HACK** If time is an issue, you can save scraps in the freezer until you're ready to re-home them. During winter, I've been known to put scraps in the kitchen freezer because it's too cold to walk out to the bokashi bin in the garage!

BUSY TIPS – WHERE TO START?

- Plan a leftover night once a week to use up food that needs to be eaten.
- Bring your own plate or container next time you're buying some sushi.
- Next time you're making dinner, double the recipe – use it for lunch or throw it in the freezer.

CLEAN

*'Our house is clean enough
to be healthy, and dirty
enough to be happy.'* – UNKNOWN

When it comes to cleaning, I'm all about balance. I want a house that looks clean, isn't going to make my kids the weird germy ones and doesn't get judged by my mother-in-law. (My MIL is awesome and would never do this, but I know some that would.) I also want to spend the least amount of time possible actually cleaning.

I don't try to fool myself that housework is some sort of joyous sensory event where I float around my home, wearing lipstick and white jeans, inhaling the scent of linen breeze. Winning to me is listening to a good crime podcast (with only one earphone in so I can hear the kids) and knocking out all my cleaning in 45 minutes with as little waste and the fewest nasty chemicals as possible.

THE MINDSET

Here's what I consider to make cleaning as quick, simple and low impact as possible.

1. Do I need it?

I've simplified the cleaning products I use a LOT. Every sink in the house used to have a myriad of bottles and sprays cluttered underneath it – a different product, scent and form for every room, surface, nook and cranny.

The products on the supermarket shelves had convinced me I needed them but, it turns out, I didn't. Now, I go for multipurpose options that I can use in all rooms and on all surfaces. I save a heap of time and money, because I'm buying so much less. There's also the mental relief of not having to navigate the jumbled chaos of bottles every time I open a cupboard.

There wasn't some landmark event, where I cleaned out every existing product in the house at once. It was far less dramatic – every time I ran out of a product, I'd ask myself if I needed to replace it. About 9.2 times out of 10, I didn't need to. (The numbers are an estimate – although I did scrape through Stage 1 Statistics at university, which I feel goes some way to validating things.)

> ⊘ **TIME HACK** Streamlining how many products you use means you're shopping a whole lot less, lugging less stuff around the house to clean with and juggling less chaos in your cupboards.

2. How is it packaged?

All of those beautiful bottles, with their colourful plastic wrappers and hard plastic spray nozzles, are a great way to make products look pretty – but, because they're made of all different types of materials, they can be tricky to recycle. Here are some easy switches I've made.

Concentrate

It's pretty common to find cleaning products in concentrated form – excess water has been taken out, meaning less packaging, transporting and impact. Just read the usage directions because we're prone to using too much concentrate, which kinda defeats the purpose.

Bulk up

Taking a bulk approach is a winner when it comes to packaging, and the good thing is that most cleaning products will last for ages, so there's a low risk of stuff going off if you stock up.

Refills

Some products come in refill form, meaning you don't have to buy a new spray trigger every time.

Most spray triggers have a universal screw thread that will fit most bottles, so give any triggers you have a good wash and reuse them on other bottles.

Use your own

Check out your local bulk store – there are lots of cleaning brands where you can refill your own bottles and containers.

> ⊘ **TIME HACK** Going for bulk and concentrated cleaning products means you're buying way less often – I love the fact that I don't have to think about cleaning products for at least six months at a time.

3. What's it made from?

For most cleaning brands, their focus is on delivering products that have the best possible user experiences. It's about the biggest bubbles, the strongest smell, the prettiest bottle – and getting us to buy more. The bummer is that, sometimes, this can be at the risk of our own health or the health of the planet. (Clearly, if a product didn't work, we wouldn't use it, but there needs to be a balance.)

The cleaning products we use get into the air we breathe, onto the surfaces we touch, and washed down our drains. Yet again, we don't fully understand the long-term impact on our own health, and the health of the environment, of using many of the ingredients around. There's also the need to further understand the synergistic effects these products have when we use them all together.

If you've ever tried to navigate a cleaning product's ingredient list, you'll know it's pretty overwhelming, and that's assuming all the ingredients have even been listed. 'Greenwashing' is also rife – when companies make misleading claims about being environmentally friendly – meaning that it's almost impossible to know if we can take the claims on packaging at face value.

I'm not after hospital-grade cleanliness, I'm after a home that's clean and healthy. I go for products with the simplest and most natural ingredients I can find. The bubbles might not be as big, and the smell might not be as strong (it's weird, but clean doesn't really have a smell – it should smell like nothing, but that's not how we've been conditioned) – but that doesn't mean anything is any less clean. It just means there are fewer nasty chemicals trying to convince me otherwise.

RE-SENSITISING YOUR NOSE When we use certain products and ingredients a lot, we can get desensitised to them, which freaks me out. I've now experienced the reverse effect – I find the smell of most traditional cleaning products really overwhelming. When I buy second-hand clothes, it takes at least three washes for the laundry powder smell to disperse enough so as to not give me a headache.

Clean doesn't have to smell of anything!

COMING CLEAN ON INGREDIENTS

Trying to navigate and keep up with ingredients can be tricky. To get you started, here are some of the biggies I try to avoid:

Optical brighteners

Found in laundry products, these coat fabric and make it appear brighter. They can cause skin irritations and also accumulate in the environment and can be toxic to fish.

PEGs (polyethylene glycols)

Used as thickeners, solvents and softeners in products such as laundry and dishwashing liquids, these also help to enhance the penetration of a product. They can be contaminated with ethylene oxide and 1,4-dioxane, both of which have been identified as possible human carcinogens.

Fun fact: PEGs are also used as a laxative in pharmaceutical products.

Phthalates

If you see the word 'fragrance' or 'parfum' on a cleaning product, it will probably have phthalates. They help fragrances linger. Studies have found phthalates to be endocrine disruptors, impacting reproductive systems. They have also been linked to asthma and allergies.

Quarternary Ammonium Compounds (Quats)

These can be used as an antimicrobial agent in products such as antibacterial wipes. Quats have been found to cause respiratory and skin irritations, and studies are exploring their potential impact on human fertility and antibiotic resistance.

Sodium laureth sulphate (SLES)

A popular surfactant, this makes things foam up and gives us those big bubbles. It can cause irritation to skin, eyes and the respiratory tract.

⊘ **TIME HACK** If you don't have time to do a chemistry degree and read through all of the ingredients, an app like Chemical Maze will do the hard work for you. Environmental Working Group is another go-to source for information on ingredients.

4. Can I do it myself?

I started this journey as a committed DIYer, replacing every cleaning product with an equivalent homemade one – I felt like I should be making things to earn my sustainability badge. But I discovered that the DIY approach didn't really work for me – I found it time-consuming, mentally and physically. I've realised that, while I like short doses of hands-on doing, my motivation comes at random times and it's not reliable enough for me to have a consistent supply of crucial things such as laundry powder.

If you are a DIY person, however, here's your chance to shine. I've included a couple of recipes from the awesome team at Figgy & Co, or you can buy 'homemade' products directly from people who make them.

> ⊘ **TIME HACK** Want homemade, but don't have the time? Convince a friend who likes making things (maybe do a swap with some baking), or buy directly from a local 'maker'.

5. Have conversations

Got a cleaner? Start a conversation with them about how you want to reduce using toxic chemicals and waste – it's better for their wellbeing, too! You may find they've got some ideas about alternatives already, and what an awesome way to create a ripple effect of change across their other clients.

> ⊘ **TIME HACK** A simple conversation will change things straight away, and you'll double down on your impact if your cleaner talks to their other clients.

GETTING IT DONE

What I use

Products and ingredients

As per the back of every cleaning product ever made – always do a patch test first.

Surface spray

I have spray bottle with a 1:1 solution of white vinegar (ideally naturally brewed) and water. I buy white vinegar in a 5 L bottle from the bulk store and refill my container when it's run out. If you're not into the smell of vinegar, leave some orange peel in the bottle for a couple of weeks.

Don't use this on natural marble or grout – instead, use the Bench Spray recipe (see page 97).

Baking soda (bicarbonate of soda)

I buy baking soda in 25 kg sacks from the bulk food store, which lasts me at least 18 months. I use food grade so I can be multipurpose with it.

Castile soap

I get one that's also suitable for using on skin so it's as multipurpose as possible.

I buy this in liquid form, and if it's made with coconut oil, I make sure it's sustainably sourced.

Oxygen bleach

Sodium percarbonate is a much gentler sanitising alternative to chlorine bleach. (Even though it's milder, it still needs to be stored and handled with care.)

MULTI-MULTIPURPOSE

The answer to almost any question in our house has become 'baking soda and white vinegar'. I love the fact that I can have two products that do so many things. Here are some of my fave uses for these wonder ingredients.

Baking soda (bicarb soda)

- Put an open container in your fridge to soak up weird smells, or sprinkle in your shoes, or anywhere else that gets stinky.
- If you spill red wine, or one of the kids (or anyone else) wees on the carpet, sprinkle with baking soda to soak it up.
- Mix with a bit of olive oil and use to rub off any sticky label residue from glass jars.
- Use with a damp cloth to rub away stains on a coffee cup.
- Clean the BBQ using a paste of baking soda and water.
- Soothe insect bites by placing some baking soda on the skin and dampening.

White vinegar

- Spray white vinegar on driveway weeds to kill them.
- No more stinky fingers! Rinse your hands with white vinegar after cutting an onion.
- Unclog your showerhead by submerging it in a bowl or plastic bag with a cup of white vinegar, and leave to soak overnight.
- Make a volcano by adding vinegar to baking soda – totally irrelevant but fun all the same!

⊘ **TIME HACK** Two products, sooo many uses. Make these the first things you buy from the bulk store – you'll get hooked.

RECIPES FROM FIGGY & CO.

If you're keen to get amongst some easy DIY recipes, I've got my mates Jane and Aimee to share a couple of their favourites. They met as paramedics and both come from medical and science backgrounds. Now they're using their incredible smarts to make the world a better place with their company, Figgy & Co. They're on a mission to make chemically conscious cleaning easy and affordable by hand-batching pared back home cleaners and supplying ingredients for you to DIY your own.

Bench spray

TO MAKE ABOUT 500 ML, YOU WILL NEED

½–1 teaspoon baking soda
500 ml water
5–10 drops essential oil, to your liking
½–1 teaspoon liquid castile soap

WHAT TO DO

1. Into a trigger bottle, combine the baking soda with a small amount of hot water to dissolve. Add the essential oil and remaining water to the solution and mix. Once combined, add the liquid castile soap and mix again.

2. For best results, give the bottle a shake before each use to activate the ingredients, then spray and wait 1–2 minutes before wiping away.

Cleaning paste

TO MAKE 2.5 CUPS, YOU WILL NEED

4 parts baking soda (2 cups)
1 part liquid castile soap (½ cup)
20 drops essential oil, to your liking

WHAT TO DO

Just add the ingredients into a bowl and stir! Add small amounts of water to loosen the mix as required. Store in an airtight container.

This is a dream to use on any hard surface, particularly in your bathroom and kitchen.

Aimee

Jane

Equipment

Cleaning cloths

I cut up old clothes that are no longer wearable – T-shirts and leggings are great for this. I remember my mum even using old undies for cleaning, but I find them awkward with all the seams, and then, of course, there's the fact that they're undies.

Cleaning brushes

Old toothbrushes are relegated to scrubbing brushes for cleaning shower corners and other small spaces. For other cleaning brushes, I go for ones made from wood that can be composted, ones with replaceable heads, or good-quality brushes that will last a long time.

Mirrors and windows

Nothing beats newspaper for streak-free drying.

NIC'S TAKE: MICROFIBRE CLEANING CLOTH SYSTEMS

There are a few different microfibre cleaning cloth 'systems' out there. Designed to be used with just water, these systems are a good way to reduce using unnecessary synthetic chemicals – win. They also embody the 'reuse' philosophy, as opposed to using disposable paper towels or cloths, which are thrown away after just a couple of uses – also win.

Be wary of falling into the trap of buying 16 different cloths for different rooms of the house however, when maybe you could have got away with one or two, plus a separate, dedicated cloth for cleaning toilets.

Also be aware that microfibre fabric is a synthetic material which, when used and washed, will shed tiny particles of microplastic. The bits are so small (hence, someone smart named them 'micro'), they tend to escape into the environment and end up in our soils, waterways and even the air. Then, in a weird twist of fate, we end up eating and drinking them – not so winning.

It's currently estimated that we're consuming 5 g (the equivalent of a credit card's weight) of microplastics every week. Mind. Blown.

The verdict

There are definitely some environmental upsides to these systems, but keep a less-is-more mindset and be mindful of the impact that those pesky little microplastics have on the planet.

Yup, I have a lot of duct tape holding my kitchen together. →

Bathroom

Baths, showers and sinks

I sprinkle baking soda over the surface then use a damp cloth to spread around, rinse and dry off.

For heavy-duty cleaning, I sprinkle oxygen bleach in the bowl, brush it around, then leave for about 30 minutes to do its thing. Another scrub and flush.

Toilet

I spray the seat with my surface spray and sprinkle baking soda all around the bowl. I leave for around 30 minutes while I do the rest of my cleaning, then give it a good scrub and wipe the spray off with toilet paper and flush. If I'm feeling a bit fancy, I'll put a couple of drops of essential oil inside the toilet paper roll.

Walls

To avoid mould, every now and then I spray problem areas with surface spray, leave for 20 minutes (or until I remember), then wipe clean and dry.

Kitchen

Sinks and bench tops

I sprinkle baking soda over the surface, then use a damp cloth to spread around, rinse and dry off. (Check the manufacturer's instructions if you have any fancy surfaces.)

Oven

Spray the inside of the oven with water to dampen, then cover with baking soda and spray again to make sure it's damp and stays in place. Leave for a few hours at least (or forget about it overnight like I do), then wipe off with a clean cloth. You do need a bit of elbow grease if you're like me and hardly ever clean your oven – but I'd rather that than getting high on some of the toxic cleaners you can use.

Dishwashing liquid

I buy a brand with clean ingredients in bulk and refill my own containers. I've also used a dishwashing bar before, which was brilliant (all the good stuff without the added water) – you just rub it between your hands in the water (or use a soap cage if you can get hold of one).

Dishwasher powder

I go for a brand with cleaner ingredients in bulk and refill my own containers. I don't use a rinse aid but, if my glasses start coming out grubby, I'll put a bowl of vinegar on the top rack during a cycle. Again, be warned that vinegar is pretty acidic, so you wouldn't want to be using it all the time because the rubber fittings won't like it.

I tried making my own, but I was rubbish at it. If you don't fancy buying or making them, find a knitter – it's an art we need to keep alive – and they'll be able to knock one out in less than an hour.

Kitchen cloths

I use knitted cotton cloths, which can be composted when they're past it. To stop them getting too manky in between washes, I pour the remains of a boiled kettle over them in my stainless steel sink.

Kitchen brushes

I go for wooden ones with natural bristles that can be composted. I also get one with a replaceable head to save needing to replace the handle. I don't have a scourer, and will instead use baking soda and a cloth if I need a bit of friction.

Floors

Vacuum

Most of what I vacuum up is food, hair, fluff and leaves – so it all ends up in the worm farm. (It's gross but the worms love it.) If you're vacuuming up plastic and other nasties, then I'd avoid composting it.

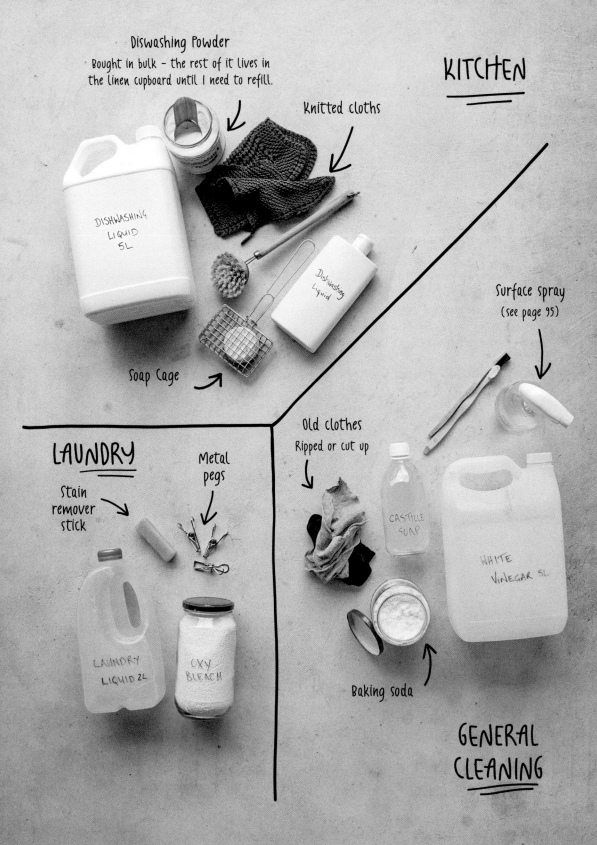

Diswashing Powder
Bought in bulk – the rest of it lives in the linen cupboard until I need to refill.

KITCHEN

Knitted cloths

DISHWASHING LIQUID 5L

Dishwashing Liquid

Soap Cage

Surface spray
(see page 95)

LAUNDRY

Metal pegs

Stain remover stick

Old clothes
Ripped or cut up

CASTILLE SOAP

WHITE VINEGAR 5L

LAUNDRY LIQUID 2L

OXY BLEACH

Baking soda

GENERAL CLEANING

Mopping

I go for hot water and a good squirt of castile soap.

Carpet

I use castile soap to spot-clean carpet (and couches); just follow instructions for dilution. To deodorise carpet, sprinkle with baking soda, leave for at least a few hours or ideally overnight, then sweep up what you can and vacuum the rest.

Laundry

Wash less often

The simplest time hack I've made is to wash our clothes less. That's gotta be a win, when I estimated that I'm going to spend more than a year doing laundry in my lifetime.

Word on the street is that we over-wash things using unnecessary water, electricity, cleaning products and, of course, time. With synthetic fabrics such as fleece, remember that these shed microplastics each time they're washed – so the less washing, the better.

I wash my clothes when they get dirty and spot-clean things if they need it. If I can get away with it, I hang things out on the line for a bit of an airing and some sunshine instead of washing them.

Let's be clear though, I'm not keen to compromise personal hygiene and will always make sure things pass the sniff test!

> ⊘ **TIME HACK** Wash your clothes less frequently. Spot cleaning or airing garments means you can save time at the washing machine.

Washing and drying

I wash at 30°C and line dry (we don't have a dryer). During winter, I put the clothes outside as much as possible and then finish them off inside when we're home in the evening.

Dry-cleaning

I try to avoid dry-cleaning as much as I can and will instead give things a light spray with vodka if they're a bit stinky.

If you still want to dry-clean, have a conversation with your dry-cleaner because there are some less chemically intensive processes, such as steam cleaning, that they may offer. Grab a reusable suit bag (it also makes you look like you're going somewhere super important), if you have one, which avoids those flimsy disposable plastic ones.

Just patch test first, and make sure you use the cheap vodka – no need to waste the good stuff.

One ear listening to a podcast, the other ear listening out for the kids.

Really need to tidy up these cords.

Pegs

I use marine-grade stainless steel pegs. They were a bit spensy, but I'm not planning on buying pegs ever again in my lifetime. They're gentle on clothes and they're awesome for clipping bags in the kitchen and building blanket forts, too.

Laundry products

Laundry liquid

I buy in bulk (enough to last me at least six months) and refill my containers. I've also purchased homemade laundry powder in bulk from a local 'maker' sold in a large paper bag.

Stain remover

I use a natural stain-removing product that comes in stick form and is packaged in a cardboard box.

Fabric softener

I don't use it. If you're into fabric softener, choose something with cleaner ingredients. Some people use vinegar but, if you're using it a lot, just be wary that some machine manufacturers advise against it due to its acidity.

Germy Jims

If we've got a tummy bug or something else funky going on, I'll use oxygen bleach in the wash as a sanitiser.

NIC'S TAKE: ESSENTIAL OILS

In addition to smelling good, essential oils are pretty magical and have some amazing properties. It feels like there's been a bit of a resurgence in interest in them via network marketing.

I think it's freaken great that people are looking at natural solutions – but you also need to watch out … just because they're natural doesn't mean they don't have a risk. (Anthrax is also natural, say no more.)

If you're keen to use them, make sure you do your research or get professional advice (aromatherapist, aromatologist, aromascience practitioner) to ensure you use them correctly. Safety first, people.

Or maybe I'm just middle-aged and that's what people my age are into so I'm noticing them more.

Windows

Confession time – I hardly ever clean my windows. (How's that for time-saving?) I normally only do it when I move house. Luckily for my windows, I've always moved reasonably frequently, but things are catching up with me now! When I do clean them, I use my surface spray and dry them off with newspaper.

The air

Beyond simplifying the products I use, there are a few other things I do to clean the air inside my home.

1. Shoes are taken off at the door. (Think about all the funky things the soles of your shoes are exposed to every day.)

2. Every day, I'll throw open a couple of windows at each end of the house to get the air moving through. Yep, even in the middle of winter – it only has to be for 5 minutes.

3. I have house plants – those things are amazing at filtering the bad stuff out of the air ($\rightarrow$ for my favourite air cleaning plants, see page 162).

4. I skip the air fresheners. Instead, I have some vanilla extract in a spray bottle ($\rightarrow$ see recipe on page 64) that I'll spritz around if I need to impress anyone.

> ⊙ **TIME HACK** Get the kids to help. Because there are no dodgy ingredients in what I'm using, when the kids are in the mood, they love getting busy around the house with the vinegar spray, or hopping in the bath or shower and giving it a scrub.

BUSY TIPS – WHERE TO START?

- Ask the socials for a recommendation of anyone local who makes natural cleaning products, and trial one.
- When you're cleaning the bath, go to the pantry and try using baking soda instead.
- Next time you're buying dishwashing liquid at the supermarket, use the Chemical Maze app or ewg.org to check the ingredients.
- Buy the biggest product size to reduce the packaging.

BEAUTY + BODY

'Inner beauty is great, but a little mascara never hurt.' — UNKNOWN

I'd love to say I shun the beauty industry, feel completely comfortable in my own skin and embrace ageing with wonder and awe … but I'm only human. (And if I run into an ex-boyfriend on the street, I don't want him to feel relieved that he got away.)

I've never been what you'd call high maintenance – but I still want to look as good as I can. I just don't want to spend a lot of time doing it. Combine that with wanting to reduce my waste and toxic load, my approach to beauty has become a whole lot simpler. My bathroom drawers are no longer an eclectic apothecary of hopes and promises – they're now home to a few simple products that I love and make me feel good.

Studies show that, on average, women spend more than 5 hours per week on their appearance.

THE MINDSET

How do I use one less product?

I don't know if you've ever noticed, but the health and beauty industry is about getting you to use more – just one more product – in what is your already complicated multistep regime. One more temptation, which promises to make your lashes longer, reduce those wrinkles or remove cellulite on a specific limb or appendage.

Trust me, I know … that was my job. Creating needs that you never knew you had, then delivering the perfect product to fix it. Convincing you that you really needed that additional product – it will make your life 94.2%* better. *Results may vary.

One of the simplest changes I've made is to flip my mindset. Instead of constantly adding in more products touted to me by marketing (which never really make my lashes 10 x longer or my skin 5 years younger), I aim to take one more product out. I'm all about simplifying my routine – this mindset saves me a heap of time and money, and means fewer ingredients and less packaging.

Comment from husband Mike: I can confirm that Nic's personal hygiene and appearance have not suffered during our lifestyle changes.

I promise I haven't 'let myself go' in the process; in fact, my skin and hair haven't been in such good condition for years.

Rolling with multipurpose products has been a massive breakthrough. Whenever I can, I'll choose options that can be used for different things, or by multiple members of the family.

What is it made from?

Ingredients

Our skin is our largest organ. On average, we have 2m² of skin (that's the same size as the large floor rug we have in our lounge), and our skin is pretty darn absorbent. We're often layering it up with a cocktail of hundreds of synthetic ingredients every day with the products we use. I'm not really down with my skin being a lab test for ingredients. Instead of waiting to see if something goes wrong, I prefer to keep things as simple as I can. My underlying philosophy is to try to only use things on my skin that I would eat.

Clearly, I wouldn't choose to eat castile soap, but I'd be okay if I did.

Even though I have a lot of edibles in my drawer (no, not that kind), there are still times when I need to navigate a product's ingredients label. There are a few biggies that I know to avoid but, sometimes, these have different names on the label, or I get confused. Along with that, the list of ingredients with risks seems to be continually getting longer.

Materials

For accessories and other 'things', I like to think about what's going to happen to them at the end of their useful lives. Cotton facecloths, a wooden hairbrush and bamboo cotton buds are destined for the compost, instead of in the bin or up a turtle's nose.

BEAUTY ALL-ROUNDERS

Here are a couple of my favourite multipurpose beauty products.

Almond oil*

With its myriad uses, almond oil is my go-to simple beauty solution.

- Face moisturiser
- Body moisturiser
- All over kids' moisturiser
- Eye make-up remover
- Beard oil (not for me)
- Nappy rash relief (also not for me)
- Kids' cradle cap removal
- Base for face scrubs
- Add it to smoothies

*Avoid if you have a nut allergy (I'm hoping that's obvious).

Jojoba and coconut oil are also great multipurpose options depending on your skin type (just skip the jojoba in your smoothie).

Castile soap

This is a vegetable-based soap, made with natural ingredients. It comes in a liquid or bar form and you can get ones that can be used for both personal care and around the house.

I always make sure I source one that only uses sustainably sourced natural ingredients, doesn't have any added synthetic dyes or perfumes. Dr Bronner's is a brilliant American brand with an amazing philosophy, but there are lots of cool local alternatives that are worth looking at, too.

I use castile soap in liquid form and dilute 1 part soap to 2 parts water and then put in a reusable foaming handwash dispenser.

I use castile soap for:

- Handwash
- Bodywash
- Facial cleanser
- Shaving foam
- Shampoo
- Household cleaners (→ see 'Clean' chapter)

⊘ **TIME HACK** Instead of constantly adding one more product to your beauty routine, try taking one out by going for multipurpose products.

NOT-SO BEAUTIFUL INGREDIENTS

It can be a mission trying to decipher ingredients labels. To keep things simple, here are a few biggies that I try to avoid:

Aluminium

Found in antiperspirants, aluminium-based compounds are used to 'plug' sweat ducts. That is enough to weird me out, given that our bodies sweat for a reason, but research is continuing to explore if there's a possible link to breast cancer and Alzheimer's disease.

Parabens

This is a preservative found in different personal care products, including make-up, deodorant, shampoo and bodywash. Studies have found possible links between parabens causing hormone disruption and an increased risk of cancer.

PEGs (polyethylene glycols)

→ For the low-down on these nasties, see page 94.

Phthalates

→ To find out about how phthalates can be hidden in ingredients lists, see page 94.

Sodium lauryl sulphate (SLS) and Sodium laureth sulphate (SLES)

These are foaming agents used to make products bubble and foam up. They can cause irritation to skin, eyes and the respiratory tract.

⊘ **TIME HACK** An app such as Chemical Maze decodes food additives and ingredients found in cosmetics, which helps me understand what it is that I'm buying and the potential risks. Thanks to Chemical Maze and the Environmental Working Group's Skin Deep Guide for all of the awesome work they do to help us navigate the ingredient minefield!

How is it packaged?

Health and beauty packaging is designed for you to buy the promise. It's about making the product stand out on the shelf, convincing you that you need it. Small intricate packaging, which is often made of many different materials, might look beautiful but can be a nightmare to recycle or reuse. It's designed to sell the product, not to reduce waste. Here are some of the options I roll with.

Package-free

I'll try to source products without packaging – one of my favourite switches is to choose things in bar form. It's not just about soap anymore. There are bars of shampoo and conditioner, moisturiser, self-tan and even deodorant. With lots of these traditional products, the major ingredient is often water – buying the product in bar form saves on the water, the excess packaging and all the impact of shipping it around.

Conditioner, Soap, Shampoo, Cleanser, Deodorant, Moisturiser...

MINUS

Aqua

EQUALS

BAR

Refilling

Being able to take your own containers and refill them is becoming more common for personal care products. Many bulk stores have products such as shampoo, conditioner, bodywash and soap on tap.

Bulking up

I buy in bulk when it makes sense. Normally, a larger bottle size means you'll reduce the overall amount of packaging (bonus points for saving time and money, too). I buy almond oil and castile soap en masse, because we use them for so many things – 1 L almond oil and 4 L castile soap last us about 18 months.

Recyclability

When choosing something that is packaged, I will opt for something that comes in recycled or recyclable packaging. If it's recyclable, I make sure it can be processed in the area I live in – and I make sure it ends up in the right bin. We're way less likely to recycle bathroom stuff.

I'm guessing it's because it's a bit further to walk to the recycling bin – or maybe that's just me?

> ⊘ **TIME HACK** Buying in bulk means that, on average, I only go shopping for beauty products once a year.

Reusable

I aim for reusability over disposability. The initial outlay will be a bit more, but you'll save in the long term. My favourite reusable switch has been moving to a safety razor, where you just replace the metal blade. I also know lots of people love the switch to reusable make-up remover pads. I just use toilet paper and almond oil – writing that down, I now realise how stingy that sounds!

> ⊘ **TIME HACK** You hardly ever need to replace reusables, so you'll spend less time shopping for them.

Do it yourself

If you're into making your own products, this is a great way to skip the packaging and know exactly what ingredients you're using. It doesn't have to be complex.
→ Read on to try the awesome facial oil recipe from my mate Sharyn, see page 116.

> ⊘ **TIME HACK** Don't have the time to DIY? Check out your local markets – all sorts of clever people are making cool things. If they don't have what you want, they'll probably be happy to whip up something for you.

EASY DOES IT Our bodies become conditioned to using certain products, and it can take a while to readjust. Instead of freaking out my skin, my hair or myself by making a dramatic switch to a new product, I've found it's better to ease myself into it. I'll either mix products together (the old product and new natural alternative) or alternate between using my existing product and my new one until my body adjusts. And don't forget the patch test!

GETTING IT DONE

Skincare

It goes without saying that we should eat well, stay hydrated, get lots of sleep and stay out of the sun at peak times (everything in moderation, though, right?)

Moisturiser

At our place, almond oil is the whole family's all-over moisturiser. My preference is to bulk-buy 1 L organic almond oil, then decant into smaller bottles. I find the best time to use it is when I first get out of the shower, because my skin is warm and will absorb it well. When I turned 40, I decided I needed to up the ante with my facial moisturiser so I moved to rosehip oil – it's also really nice, but didn't magically make my skin 5 years younger, and was just one more thing to think about, so I've reverted to almond oil.

Facewash

I use a few drops of castile soap and a knitted cotton facecloth. When I feel like my face needs it, I grab some spent coffee grounds and almond oil to make a scrub (you can also use white or brown sugar; I tried oats once – it felt nice, but I wasn't down with a face full of porridge).

NINJA HERBAL-INFUSED OILS

Herbal-infused oils are an awesome way to nourish your skin naturally.

My mate Sharyn is a mum to two young boys, and a plant and herbal ninja. She started Plant and Share, which creates natural skincare inspired by the plants and preparations our ancestors have used for centuries. What I love about Sharyn is that she's all about sharing her ideas and knowledge to help other people do things better for themselves.

Here's her recipe for lavender herbal oil, which she calls an excellent 'everything' oil with heaps of benefits. Use it as a moisturiser, massage oil, bath oil or make-up remover.

Lavender herbal oil

YOU WILL NEED

Sterilised jar with clean lid (size depends on what you have available)

Clean cheesecloth or muslin (for straining)

Carrier oil (enough to fill your jar) (avoid rancid oils, or ones close to their expiry date). Good options include:

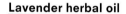

- Sunflower (*Helianthus annuus*) – good lightweight oil for sensitive skin
- Olive (*Olea europaea*) – better for dry skin

Large bunch of dried lavender (find some in a 'garden near you' and hang to dry in a warm dark place)

Vitamin E capsule (optional – acts as an antioxidant)

SHARYN'S TIP Patch test oil on a small area of skin first and, in the unlikely event of a reaction, discontinue use and consult a medical practitioner. Only apply herbal oils externally and keep out of reach of children.

WHAT TO DO

1. Strip or coarsely chop your lavender or put in a food processor (the finer the pieces, the better).

2. Loosely fill your sterilised jar with the lavender. Pour over the carrier oil until all the lavender is covered and there are no air pockets. Screw on the lid and shake.

3. Store in a warm, dark place (on a plate because some oil may leak out). Leave for 4–6 weeks, giving it a shake when you remember and checking for mould.

4. Strain the oil, add the contents of the vitamin E capsule if using and return to its original jar for another 24 hours to allow the sediment to settle.

5. Pour oil into dark-coloured glass bottles and use within a year.

Make-up

Foundation
I use a natural beauty balm (BB) cream, which comes in a reusable and recyclable metal tin.

Eyes
I use a natural mascara that comes in a reusable and recyclable metal tin, and a pencil eyeliner (and compost the shavings).

Bronzer
I use straight cocoa powder. Yep, for real – it took me a while to trial this because I'm not really a cocoa complexion … I started by mixing some cocoa with my existing bronzer and slowly transitioned.

Cost for a year's supply of cocoa bronzer = NZ$0.50.

> ⊘ **TIME HACK** When I run out, I just have to go to the pantry instead of the department store.

Lips and cheeks
I use a natural option that comes in a reusable and recyclable metal tin. I keep hold of the metal tins, because my daughter likes making lip balms and giving them as gifts.

Cotton buds

I use cotton buds for make-up application and removal. I've switched to bamboo or paper alternatives that can end up in the compost bin.

Sunscreen

I use natural sunscreens where the active ingredient is zinc oxide (Yep, the old-school paint-on zinc made famous by surf life-savers in the '80s). They are a bit thicker to rub on, but the ingredients are normally a lot cleaner. I get sunscreen in a cardboard tube – it's easier to paint on, and it can be composted. Look for products that are:

- Broad spectrum
- Minimum of SPF 30
- Meets AS/NZS 2604 standard
- Reef-safe (doesn't contain oxybenzone and octinoxate)

Cleaning yo' self

Bodywash and hand soap

We use liquid castile soap diluted 1 part soap to 2 parts water, kept in foaming handwash pumps. The foaming pump makes it really nice to use and it goes so much further – I'm pretty sure my family used to pour bodywash straight down the drain based on how much we went through. I reuse plastic foaming pump bottles bought from the supermarket years ago (or check if any of your friends have some that are destined for the recycling bin).

You can buy fancy ceramic bottles if you want – but I highly recommend plastic ones, if you have small children or are slightly uncoordinated like me.

Deodorant

There is no such thing as a natural antiperspirant – stopping yourself sweating is not a natural process. I use a solid deodorant bar that comes in a cardboard tube and, for lighter days, use a crystal rock (a natural mineral salt that you moisten and rub under your armpits). I paid NZ$7.65 for mine 4 years ago and reckon I'll get another 12 years out of it. If you are a regular antiperspirant user, consider doing an armpit detox when making the switch – yep, it's really a thing!

Perfume

I go for a brand that uses essential oils and natural botanicals with no added synthetic ingredients. If you're using an essential-oil-based perfume, make sure you're buying from someone who knows what they're doing.

Haircare

Cleaning

Shampooing

Mike and the kids use castile soap to wash their hair.

I used to wash and condition my hair every day. I now do it every 5–7 days, using a shampoo bar. What gets me through between washes is dusting cornflour through my roots with an old make-up brush – it acts like a dry shampoo.

> ⊘ **TIME HACK** It sounds ridiculous, but saving 10 minutes in my morning routine by not washing my hair every day is a freaken game changer.

Conditioning

For conditioning, my daughter and I use an apple cider vinegar rinse, which is 1 part vinegar to 2 parts water.

Vinegar is an odour neutraliser so I promise you won't smell like a bag of chips. You can add some orange peel for a few weeks before using, if you'd prefer a citrus scent. Also works great as a deterrent for head lice.

Styling

If I ever need a styling product, I make up a sugar spray (dissolve 1 tablespoon sugar in half a cup of warm water and spray on) – it works like a light hairspray. (Maybe just avoid standing next to a beehive.)

Hair salons

I get my hair coloured at the salon a few times a year – man, it makes me feel good, and it's not something I'm willing to give up! I go to a salon that does a lot to reduce its waste, and that uses organic and ammonia-free products.

> @ **FIND IT ONLINE** Check out sustainablesalons.org – this is a service that beauty and hair salons use to help them divert their waste. They do things like collecting cut hair and using it to make 'hair booms', which soak up oil spills.

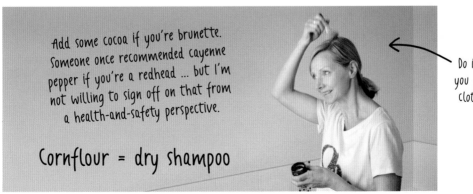

Add some cocoa if you're brunette. Someone once recommended cayenne pepper if you're a redhead ... but I'm not willing to sign off on that from a health-and-safety perspective.

Cornflour = dry shampoo

Do it before you put your clothes on.

Safety
Razor

All-in-one
man bar

Shaving
brush

Hair removal

Razors

Both my husband and I have switched to using safety razors (we each have our own ones, we're not that close). While initial outlay for the handle is more, they work out a lot cheaper in the long run and, from a waste perspective, all you replace is the steel razor blade when it blunts. You do need to slow down a bit when you use them (there was an incident when I first made the switch), but they do a great job.

Mike's input: 'I love my safety razor – it takes a bit of getting used to, but it gives a great shave, and I'm not having to replace the blade any more frequently than I was before.' In case you're wondering, he's qualified – he is a very hairy man.

Other hair removal

- Laser is a great option for permanent hair removal – it'll set you back a chunk of cash and only works on certain skin and hair tones, but it's worth looking into.
- Threading is something a couple of my mates swear by for their eyebrows and upper lips. You could even ask to take the cotton home to compost, if you were into it. Too far?

Shaving foam

For shaving, I use the foaming castile soap. Mike uses a solid bar, which he lathers up: it's an all-in-one man bar – shampoo, facewash, bodywash and shaving foam in one – a perfect example of how we don't really need all of those different products!

Teeth

Toothbrushes

We've made the switch to bamboo toothbrushes. Once they're finished with, I use them as cleaning brushes or garden markers. Ultimately, they can be composted – just be sure to remove the bristles, contain these and put them in the rubbish.

Once I have a stockpile, I grab a pair of pliers and a glass of wine, and get plucking.

> ⊘ **TIME HACK** Some people just snap the heads off bamboo toothbrushes and throw that bit away – it's still way less waste overall.

We also have an electric toothbrush that is 11 years old. I'm not going to stop using it and throw it out … it already exists and I'm going to use that sucker until it dies.

Toothpaste

We use a combination of conventional toothpaste (I just use Chemical Maze to help on the ingredients) and a natural tooth powder in a jar. Most natural toothpastes don't contain fluoride and I'm a complete fence-sitter when it comes to the fluoride debate, so I use a bit of both. Also coming onto the market now are chewable 'tooth tablets' – they tick the low-waste box and I'm hanging out to hear whether they're a legit option from a dental-health perspective. Check out terracycle.com for toothpaste tube recycling.

Get advice from your dentist – those docs know teeth.

Toilet paper

Linen that we actually use (80% got axed)

Bulk almond oil

Bulk pantry overflow

Laundry refill

Bulk pantry overflow

Dental floss

Conventional dental floss is often plastic-coated and has artificial flavouring – Boo! We've switched to a natural, compostable option that comes in a refillable container.

Sanitary protection

I use a menstrual cup, along with reusable pads and period underwear. Wow, does it save a lot of cash! Menstrual cups do take a bit of getting used to, but not ever having to buy tampons again is liberating! If you're not yet up for reusables, it's all good – I'd recommend switching to an unbleached and organic product if you can – and never flush those guys down the toilet, as they cause all sorts of plumbing issues.

Toilet paper

We order paper-wrapped toilet paper on a three-monthly subscription basis. The subscription saves time and I never have to think about buying toilet paper again. There are heaps of options for switching to lessen the impact: unbleached, unperfumed, unwrapped, Forestry Stewardship Council certified, double length, locally manufactured, recycled ...

You can go all out and switch to a bidet or use reusable wipes (aka 'family cloth') – you'll be way more hard-core than I am.

> ⊘ **TIME HACK** Subscription services for things like toilet paper are a great time saver. Ordering in bulk will help reduce the transport impact.

Paper wrappers and toilet rolls are used for craft, wrapping paper, growing plant seedlings and, ultimately, they're composted. (My daughter often grabs the recycling bin for her arts and craft projects.)

> ⊘ **TIME HACK** The delivery of a big box filled with 48 rolls of colourfully wrapper toilet paper amuses my kids for a good couple of hours of play – it's almost worth it for that alone.

First-aid kit

Medicines

This is something I don't muck around with – if we need medicines, I get them. If there's a better choice from a packaging perspective, or if I can get a smaller pack size when we don't need the full quantity prescribed, then I'll go for that – but I don't tie myself up in knots about waste if it's necessary.

Home remedies

Whenever we have minor ailments in the house, instead of going out to buy a product, my first step is to do a quick internet search for natural home remedies. Most of the time, I find that we have something around the house that will do the trick.

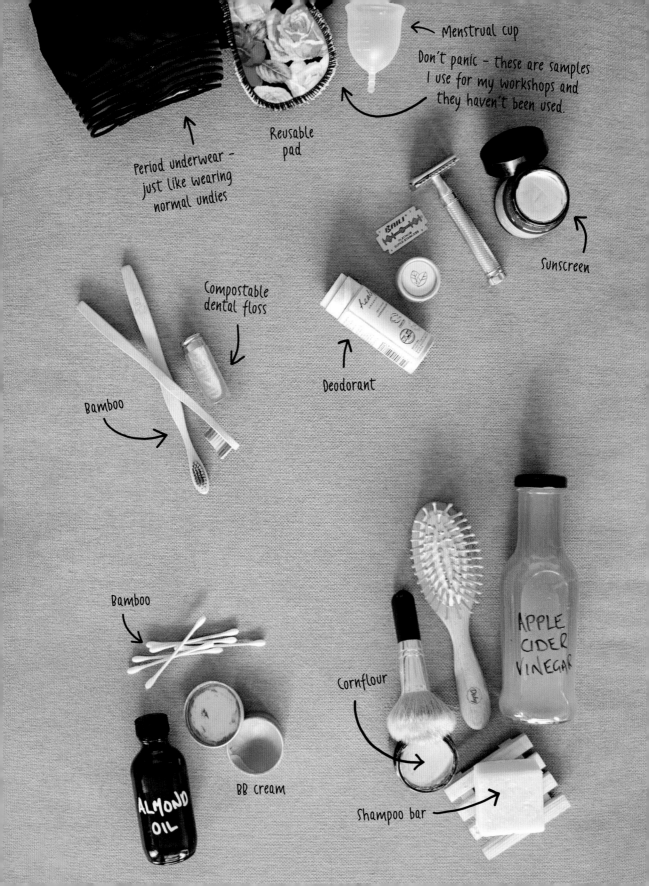

Menstrual cup

Don't panic - these are samples I use for my workshops and they haven't been used.

Reusable pad

Period underwear - just like wearing normal undies

Sunscreen

Compostable dental floss

Deodorant

Bamboo

Bamboo

Cornflour

APPLE CIDER VINEGAR

BB cream

ALMOND OIL

Shampoo bar

MY GO-TO HOME REMEDIES

Sore throats
- We use a saltwater gargle = 1 teaspoon of salt in ½ cup warm water

Minor coughs and colds
- Lemon honey drinks
- Steamy showers
- Ginger tea (using fresh ginger)
- Hankies or toilet paper for noses

Insect bites
- Apply a paste of baking soda (bicarb soda) and water, or a few drops of apple cider vinegar.

Mild burns
- Run under cold water, then apply aloe vera gel squeezed out straight from the plant.

⊙ **TIME HACK** Going for home remedies means you save time by not shopping for other products. They seem to work, but if they don't, the placebo effect is often enough to make everyone feel better.

Plasters

We have big rolls of paper surgical tape and cotton gauze that we use when we need a plaster. It lasts for years!

⊙ **TIME HACK** Tackle one product at a time – each time I'm about to run out of a product, that's my trigger to see if there's a better switch I can make.

BUSY TIPS – WHERE TO START?
- Ask for a sampler pack of shampoo and conditioner bars for your next birthday and see what works for you.
- If you've got some almond oil in the cupboard, give it a whirl as an eye make-up remover or a moisturiser.
- Next time you buy a product and want to check the ingredients, use the Chemical Maze app or check out ewg.org.
- Find a brand or a retailer with products and ingredients that you trust and make it your go-to source.

OUT AND ABOUT

'Wherever you go,
there you are.' – **CONFUCIUS**

It's pretty common for our lives, work and wanderlust to be scattered all over the show – we want and need to get around and spend time in other places. We need to get to where we're going and get stuff done within the juggle of everyday life. Here's how I lessen my impact when I'm getting around.

THE MINDSET

Whenever I'm going somewhere, I make sure I apply my approach of mindful consumption to what I'm doing and where I'm going. Whether it's in the workplace, on holiday or just being out and about doing everyday things, it's simply about being conscious and making better choices where I can.

GETTING IT DONE

Day to day

Each day, before I leave the house, I'll try to stop and think about what I'm doing and what I need to take to be prepared. I don't always remember or get it right, however, so I have a stash of stuff in my car and handbag as a back-up.

Inside my handbag

or man bag

My handbag goes with me everywhere, so I have a few basics to keep me covered. I can fit everything in, but it does get a bit bulky and I'll tend to offload my cup and my bottle onto my desk, my bike basket or my car.

Here's what's in my regular stash:
• Drink bottle and coffee cup – I'll throw these in when I leave the house
• A fold-up shopping bag and a couple of produce bags
• A metal straw
• A hankie or a couple of muslin cloths, for wiping kids or hands
• If I know I need it, I'll throw a container in another bag, or will just grab a plate from the office.

If you want something in your handbag all the time, get yourself a collapsible container that folds up pretty small.

I don't change my handbag regularly (I only have two and one is for going out for a special occasion) but, if you do, you can always put everything in a drawstring bag and just transfer this between handbags.

Inside my car

My car is way more than a mode of transportation – it's often my office, the kids' changing room, a place to eat meals (I was one of those people who said I'd never let my kids eat in the car … and then I had kids). Because it's a space that's used for all sorts of things, and takes us all sorts of places, it's good to be prepared.

Shopping bags

I always have a couple of shopping bags in the back seat with some produce bags in them. I know some people who keep a washing basket in their car for carrying their supermarket shopping (bloody genius).

Take home for worms.

T.P. – for cleaning on the go

Picnic set

I have a backpack with a picnic blanket, cutlery, plates, containers and a bottle opener (don't drink and drive, people!) that lives in the boot of the car.

Coffee cup and drink bottle

I'm in the habit of always walking out the door with mine, but some people prefer to have spare ones that stay in the car. Empty coffee cups are handy for storing banana skins and other food scraps, so I can take them home to be composted without stinking out the car.

Roll of toilet paper

Yep, I've just realised how random that is – I use loo roll for wiping kids, containers, cups and lots of other things. I can then just throw it straight in the compost when I get home.

My friend Andrea has six reusable coffee cups that she distributes between home, work and handbag to make sure she always has one handy.

Choosing your ride

Almost every sustainability campaign I've ever come across has told me that, to help save the planet, I should be using my car less and using my bike, feet and public transport more. Of course, this is the right thing to do, but it's always seemed like a bit of a romantic notion.

It felt like sustainable transport was for other people, people who weren't always having to rush to places like I was. It was for people with less busy lives. But then, I started thinking differently – what if I could make it part of the juggle, instead of another thing to try to squeeze in?

Incidental exercise

I used to carve time out of my week to exercise. This normally involved getting in my car and driving to the gym to work out, then driving home again. Instead of seeing exercise as a separate (and rather time-consuming) activity – how could I make it part of what I was already doing?

Most days now, I walk or cycle the kids to school and pre-school, then pick up the pace and carry on to the office. I'll always choose the stairs over the lift, too. Yep, it takes a bit longer than driving but, man, it puts everyone in a good headspace, and most days I get enough exercise to skip the gym. The best thing about this is that it doesn't make exercising feel like a big deal. Some days, I still need a good blowout at the gym or a yoga class, but I love the fact that I'm getting regular exercise outside and have become one of those people who rides a bike with a basket.

My friend Sean is a cyclist and he once told me 'There's no such thing as bad weather, just bad gear' – but I'm not quite that hard-core. If the weather is really bad, I'll take the car. I reckon I end up biking or walking at least 70% of the time, and I'm pretty stoked with that.

> ⊘ **TIME HACK** Jumping on my bike or beating the feet for my daily commute means I can spend less time at the gym.

The adventure

With kids, I've learned to make the journey part of the adventure. A weekend walk to the farmers' market is as much fun as the market itself – even more so if it rains, or autumn leaves are around. A bus trip to anywhere is the highlight of the weekend. Sometimes it's niggly, it takes a bit longer, or somebody throws their toys, but the kids love it and, if I shift my thinking to see it as an experience, I'm into it, too.

Cars

Recently, we needed to replace one of our cars and we went full electric. It's a basic model that is about five years old. It seriously feels like we're driving the future, and I love the fact I never need to go to a petrol station. The car has a range of about 100 km and, to recharge it, we just plug it into a normal power point in the garage. It works for about 80% of the trips we do – we still need a second car and we use that one for longer trips.

Electric cars are a great choice in NZ, where the bulk of the electricity comes from renewable sources.

When we need to replace our other car, we'll choose a hybrid. It's a no-brainer – with standard hybrids, you don't even need to plug them in because all the charging happens while you're driving (it's something to do with the motherboard or the flux capacitor – well, that's my take on it). You'll hardly even notice the difference from a petrol car – you'll be using less petrol and, sometimes, they'll be weirdly quiet.

> @ **FIND IT ONLINE** Car sharing is also a great option. Jump online and search for car sharing apps in your area. There are also platforms that allow you to borrow from private owners (or you could list your own car to share). When you realise how much time your car just sits around, waiting to be driven, it's a pretty smart idea.

Public transport

There are not a lot of public transport options in our small town but, whenever I'm travelling in a big city, I'll use public transport as much as I can. I love the fact that you can read a book or watch the world go by, while somebody else takes care of the driving. The people-watching is also pretty fun, too.

Planes

Plane travel is having a massive impact on the planet, and the amount we're flying is continuing to increase at a freakish rate. It's a big part of modern life – and something I know I couldn't go cold-turkey on. But I've found that by flipping my mindset to think about how I can fly a bit less I've reduced my impact, which feels really good, and it's often saved me time and money.

I never used to think twice before booking a flight on a plane. Now I do. I still fly places, but I'm more conscious about the decisions I make.

If I'm travelling for work, I'll see if I can substitute with a virtual meeting or I'll make the most of any trip by running extra events or booking in additional meetings.

When I book my plane ticket, I'll opt to pay the extra for the carbon offset option – every little bit helps. (Most airlines have this available through their booking systems.)

Taking a break

In a perfect world, we would all be avid staycationers, spending our annual leave planting native saplings and restoring local wetlands. But if that's not for you, fear not – there are a heap of simple things we can do to lessen our impact when it comes to holidays. The awesome thing is that it's not about taking more time, it's about being consistent and having the right mindset.

Keep up your habits

I love going away on holiday and falling out of my normal routines and habits – hello holiday eating and afternoon naps. But I've also found that there's a temptation to fall into the social norms of what's going on around us, and it's not always a good thing – like being surrounded by other tourists drinking out of disposable water bottles and thinking, what's just one more bottle? When you're heading away from your natural habitat, shifting your mindset to be more conscious of your habits will be a massive win.

Pick your place

Destination

I'm a huge fan of travel – and I love exploring new places. We don't go overseas nearly as often as we used to (young kids and a carbon conscience will do that to you), we're more into exploring locally. When we do go overseas, we'll make the most of it by staying in one place longer and going deeper (instead of trying to cover as much territory as we can in a short amount of time).

Where to stay

- Food: When I'm picking accommodation, I'll favour places with some sort of kitchen facilities. This means we have more choice about how we eat, which saves us a heap of money and waste. I'll also see if I can find somewhere with a local market nearby. This is a cool way to get amongst fresh, local and package-free food.
- Location: I'll choose places that are close to most things or have easy access to public transport.
- Waste set-up: Before booking, I ask if they have recycling and composting – yep, I'm that person. I've been pleasantly surprised at how many places have engaged with me in the conversation.
- Use less: I'll hang up our towels and skip the daily housekeeping. I'll avoid those mini toiletries and move them, so it's obvious we didn't use any. I also ask for real milk – it tastes way better and skips the tiny little plastic containers.

If the place doesn't have composting, I've been known to bring my food scraps home after a weekend away – too far?

WHAT TO PACK

Clothes

Like most people, I used to massively over pack when it came to clothes and shoes. Now, I only pack my favourites – because that's all I end up wearing.

Reusables

- Drink bottle – if needed, I'll take a UV water purifier – this ingenious little stick contraption means you never need to buy bottled water again.
- Reusable container – handy for packed lunches and takeaways
- Coffee cup
- Cutlery – just put anything sharp in your checked luggage.
- Produce bags – for shopping at markets, buying bread and carrying random things that the kids collect
- Muslin cloths – with a bit of water, these work as a wet wipe for kids' hands and faces, and I can wipe out and reuse cups and containers.

Most things fit inside each other Russian Doll–style and get carried in a backpack.

In-flight items

- Snacks in reusable containers – I'll normally cancel my meal on a flight and, if I'm organised, pre-pack something or grab some sushi in my container from the airport (be mindful about possible quarantine issues with taking food off the plane at your destination).
- Drink bottle – if you take your bottle to the kitchen during the flight, one of the staff will fill it up from a large drum of drinking water.
- Coffee cup – coffee tastes so much better than out of the disposable ones.
- Headphones – mine are more comfortable and it saves on the plastic-wrapped ones.
- Pashmina – folds up small in my bag and means I can skip the plastic-wrapped blanket (and it smells like home, not weird commercial cleaning products).
- Toiletries – I take things in bar form when I can. These are so much lighter and less leaky than bottles of stuff.
- Paperwork – go digital. I take photos of things on my phone, or download the relevant apps.

What to bring home

Grandma went to Timbuktu and all she brought me was this T-shirt ...

When we're away, our family does things instead of buying things – photos and videos are a zero-wasters dream.

If I want to bring something for people back home, I'll choose presents that are locally made, good quality or consumable (local booze is a favourite). When I'm away, I'll also try to track down second-hand shops – you can get your hands on some awesome local finds and it gets you off the beaten track.

I love travelling with a bag that's half the size of what it used to be – not only does it lessen the impact of flight emissions, it's way easier to get around with.

My packing inspiration comes from McGyver (yup, my childhood TV hero who could multipurpose the hell out of anything he had on hand). I like to pack a few versatile items that I can do lots with – it's all stuff I use on a daily basis.

⊘ **TIME HACK** Pack your bag and then take out half the clothes – trust me!

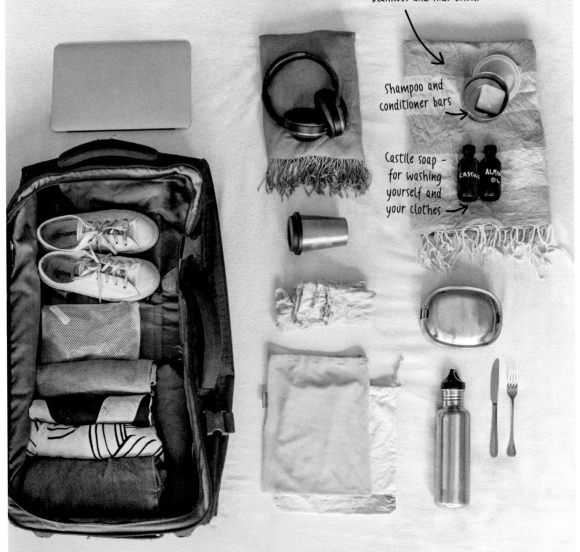

Cotton Turkish towels double as sarongs, picnic blankets and kids linen.

Shampoo and conditioner bars

Castile soap – for washing yourself and your clothes

DOING THE WORK

From home admin to big city corporate gigs, we all have work to get done. Whether it's ordering family Christmas presents online or running a conference, the same thinking applies when it comes to reducing your impact.

Create a new norm

The freaken exciting news is that if we're working in an organisation or with other people, there's also a huge opportunity to create a ripple effect of change.

It's human nature to want to fit in. (*Try standing backwards in a lift!*) We're influenced by social norms, meaning we look to people around us to inform our decisions and our behaviour. No one wants to feel like the weirdo at work, handing over a container when everyone else is getting their takeaways in disposables, or pulling out their own personal Bokashi bin from under their desk. But, if you've already nailed behaviours in your personal life, back yourself and do it at work. Just do you, and you might create a new norm.

> **TUPPERWARE GIRL** My friend Sharon (not her real name, but this was the name I wanted when I was 10 years old, thanks to watching too much *Neighbours*) works for a big corporate company. She was in the habit of carrying a collapsible container in her handbag on the weekends when she was out and about with the kids, and decided to start taking it to the in-house café at her work. She earned the nickname 'Tupperware girl' … and embraced it.
>
> Six months on, and her office now has a container library, the café offers a discount for people bringing their own takeaway containers, and heaps of staff are getting into it. *The ripple effect in action.*

CONTAINER LIBRARY

It's nice to share

Co-working

I love working from a shared office space. Because I work for myself, I love going to a place where I can feel sociable and talk to other people. It's also a bloody smart way to share resources and avoid unnecessary office stuff and waste – from stationery and printers to coffee machines and electricity, it just makes sense.

Share stuff

Rather than every person needing their own stapler, ruler, pencil sharpener and hole punch, share things instead. I've worked in offices where there's a station of communal resources. Just don't be that person who uses the last staple.

At my co-working space, there's a stash of containers and reusable cups in the kitchenette, which people can grab when they're heading out to get something. Normally, I'll grab a plate or crockery cup – I love the way it makes me feel like I'm eating homemade food.

One time, I brought a bowl to get soup from the café down the street – I learned then that a container with a lid was a way smarter choice.

> ⊘ **TIME HACK** You don't even need to remember your reusables, just use what's in the cupboard at work.

Work with others

We're all in this together, and instead of trying to crack it on our own, it can really help to work together. It can be as simple as partnering with a neighbouring business to have a joint worm farm or sharing a ride to work with a colleague.

I once offered one of the guys from the co-working space a ride on my bike's handlebars, but he wasn't into it.

SYSTEMS & SET UP

Whether you're in your home office or working in a sprawling cubicle maze with lots of others, create the path of least resistance to make it as easy as possible to do the right thing.

- Take your rubbish bin out from under your desk to avoid the temptation of just throwing things in there. It changes the 'path of least resistance' and makes you more likely to recycle or compost things.
- Make sure recycling bins are clearly labelled and easy to navigate.
- I've worked in offices where there's been a table of reusable coffee cups and containers right by the front door, or where we've given the local café a stash to keep behind the counter to help people remember to use them.
- Have systems set up to make sure things get reused (our co-working space has a box under the printer for scrap paper that can be reused).

OFFICE SUPPLIES

- I'll look at the whole lifecycle of something when I'm purchasing it. I'll think about what it's made from, how long it will last and what will happen to it at the end of its useful life – when it's cheaper to replace a whole printer rather than the toner cartridges, I get a bit fired up.

- I'll choose to buy from suppliers that have a sustainability focus and are doing the right things to reduce their own impact. (If I had a formal procurement policy, I'd give waste and sustainability a significant weighting.)

- Whenever I order something, I'll ask about how it's packaged and if there's a way to avoid any single-use plastics.

- I'll go for reusables over disposables – such as refillable fountain pens or highlighter pencils (where the shavings can be composted).

- Instead of giving out business cards, I'll grab someone's number or email address, and send them a message there and then – I've found it a way more effective way of connecting. If someone offers me a business card, I'll take a photo of it and hand it back. I know that won't work for some business cultures, so read the situation and do what feels right.

- I go for second-hand furniture and refurbished electronics.

Check out organisations like allheartnz.org.nz that
do amazing things re-homing corporate furniture.

All of this stuff is relevant, whether you work in a big company with a massive procurement team, or you're a one-man-Sam business, or if you're just sourcing stuff for home. Don't overthink things though, once you've got the right mindset, it applies no matter what the scale.

Go digital

I've heard of law firms that have reduced their paper usage by more than 90% by using digital technology – yep, law firms. If they can do it, anyone can – they just love paper filing.

Communication

Pretty much anything that I send out or receive is now electronic – bank statements, invoices and newsletters. If I get any 'admin' sent in the post I'll contact the sender straight away and see if there's a way to switch to a virtual option.

Having an electronic family calendar shared with my husband is hands down the best life hack we've ever made.

Meetings and notes

I take my laptop with me to meetings and use the electronic version of notes and presentations. If I need to really concentrate on reading something detailed, I find I still have to print it off – I just make sure it's double-sided and black-and-white (have this set as the default on your printer's settings – path of least resistance and all).

Planning

I use my phone to write notes, and for list apps and calendars. I share these with whoever needs access to stuff at work or home.

Packages and post

Sending parcels

Reuse packaging that you already have. There are now a number of courier companies that let you use your own packaging and print off your own labels. And check out some of the awesome home compostable options that are available.

> ⊘ **TIME HACK** No more going to the post office to buy special one-use plastic bags.

Incoming packages

Whenever I order something, I always add a request in the 'special instructions' field for the supplier to reuse packaging they have, to save on single-use plastic. My favourite parcel was a book that arrived in a Shapes cracker box, and was ← *The kids were gutted it wasn't actually biscuits.* padded with biscuit wrappers.

Promotional materials

If you receive catalogues, magazines or newsletters that you don't read (you know, those plastic-wrapped glossy magazines that end up in a pile on your bench or desk), unsubscribe from them, or see if there's a digital option. If you have a letterbox, make sure you have a friendly 'no circulars' sign.

> ⊘ **TIME HACK** Getting sent less crap in the mail means less time feeling guilty about not reading it and saves time continually sorting out a pile of mail.

BUSY TIPS – WHERE TO START?

- Choose a nice day to skip the gym, then bike or walk to where you're going instead.
- If you're booking a flight and don't need the meal, cancel it and save the waste.
- Next time you're going out for sushi, grab a plate from the office kitchen.
- Put some reusable produce bags (or a few of the plastic supermarket bags that you have stuffed in a kitchen drawer) in your handbag or man bag now – yep, now. Do it.

ALL YOU NEED IS LESS

'Trying to be happy by accumulating possessions is like trying to satisfy hunger by taping sandwiches all over my body.' – ROGER J CORLESS

Let's make this clear – I don't live in a one-room yurt that's decorated with only homespun alpaca wool wall-hangings and driftwood dream catchers. I appreciate nice things, and I have some stuff, just not nearly as much as I used to. I've come to the realisation that accumulating more and more stuff doesn't bring me incremental happiness. Striving for the elusive 'more' takes up a heap of time, is a bit empty and isn't great for the planet.

I want a simpler life that's not overrun by stuff. I don't want the things I have to define me or take up all my time and energy. I want the right amount of stuff to make my life enjoyable and comfortable, without it compromising my own wellbeing or the wellbeing of the planet. I've reconnected to the value of things and want to teach my kids the same philosophy.

Changing my relationship with stuff has been a pretty fascinating adventure. I've read, watched, followed, experimented, failed ... and won. From there, I've carved out my own hybrid approach that works within the realities of my life.

What follows is my mixed tape of ideas and tools to help you design your own journey towards owning less but gaining so much more.

THE MINDSET

Changing our relationship with stuff is more than just decluttering and getting rid of things. I've found that also being conscious of how stuff keeps coming in, and how it goes out, is the best way for me to keep the balance. Shifting my mindset has meant connecting with what I buy and what I have.

Feel the love

In a time when anything we want is merely a click away, it feels like we've lost the love. We need to love what we have, and break up with the love of having more, newer, bigger and better. It's about slowing our consumption.

Too much is a waste

Most things don't hold their value either. →

I have a philosophy of setting things free. (My brother didn't agree with my thinking when I let all the birds out of his aviary.) To me, having things sit in a cupboard, never being used, seems a waste. I'd way rather they were out in the world with someone who will use them. If someone can have mine, it will also stop them from having to buy something new, and that saves bringing more stuff into the world.

How much is enough?

I believe in only having things that serve a purpose (like a grater) or that I love. I don't have a fixed number, but a philosophy that helps me figure out what my 'enough' is.

My concept of what's enough is constantly evolving and reducing. As I started living with less, I realised how much it simplifies things and brings a certain ease to life. Not in a weird way, but in a simpler, lighter kinda way. From reducing the money I was spending, to saving time with less tidying, organising and maintaining, along with also reducing the emotional overwhelm, decision fatigue and environmental impact. Less feels good.

We've all got our own personal level of enough – we just need to tune into it.

Trade Me estimates that in NZ there are 73 million items sitting in people's homes and garages that aren't being used.

GETTING IT DONE

MINDSET

STEP ONE → **STEP TWO** → **STEP THREE**

Getting to less | What comes in | Letting things go

Have only things that you love or serve a purpose. | Be conscious of what and how much you let in. | Make mindful choices about where stuff goes when you've finished with it.

Step One: Getting to less

Decluttering has become a trend, a fad, a movement. Call it what you will, it's a thing – which, in itself, is pretty freaky. We now have so much stuff that there's a whole 'thing' dedicated to helping us get on top of it. There are a heap of cool people and approaches out there that will give you the tools to get on top of things.

As with everything, it's pretty personal; you need to find the right approach that helps you navigate things in a way that works for you. Here's my take on a few of the main decluttering approaches.

Marie Kondo (the KonMari™ method)

Oh, Marie, how I love your gentle and ritualistic Japanese ways! Her structured room-by-room approach is a lovely 'paint by numbers' way to tackle stuff on a household level. I'm a big fan of her direction to engage with every possession you have, asking yourself if it 'sparks joy' in you. It feels a little eccentric to begin with, but it helps you tune into the things that you really love. I swoon at her philosophy of respecting the items that you have – talking to them, caressing them with her infamous folding techniques and thanking them for their 'service'.

The verdict

KonMari can feel a bit out there, and is best served with a sense of humour *or a glass of sav* – but I'm totally into the fact that this approach is about loving and valuing what we have.

Minimalism

Some people become overwhelmed or alienated by the minimalism concept, thinking they can only own three shoes, half a couch and a Swiss army knife. If you consider minimalism as being a competition to have the fewest things possible, then I reckon you're missing the point. And if you get too obsessive about it, there's a risk no one will want to invite you over to dinner for fear of being judged for having too many scatter cushions.

I'm into minimalism from the perspective of freeing yourself from the things you don't need. I love the fact that it's about getting rid of unnecessary stuff so we can spend our time and energy on other things. I'm a fan of using this approach to make intentional choices about what we have, as opposed to letting our consumption just roll over us.

I thanked my denim jacket from the '90s for all the good times we had together, then sent it on its way to find a new friend to have adventures with. It was weirdly cathartic.

30-DAY MINIMALISM CHALLENGE

Here's the idea:
- **Day 1: Get rid of one item**
- **Day 2: Get rid of two items**
- **Day 3: Get rid of three items, and so on**

By the end of 30 days, you'll have gotten rid of 465 things. This approach can be an easy way to get started and gather some momentum. It works better if you do it with friends, or if you can join an online challenge and do it with virtual strangers. A little bit of accountability and some healthy competition can go a long way.

@ **FIND IT ONLINE** Check out theminimalists.com/game/ for the rules of the game and to find a friend … or a bit of competition.

This pillowcase was mine as a child.

KonMari folding method

Items that can't be folded go in boxes or containers.

Bottoms in this drawer

Tops in this drawer

The Packing Party approach

I still do this sometimes – it's a nice safety net if you're not sure you're ready to get rid of certain things.

Two guys called The Minimalists talk about the concept of 'The Packing Party' – one of them boxed up everything in his home and stored it in one room. Over a three-week period, he took out anything he needed. At the end of the time, he found that 80% of the things he owned stayed boxed up. As a result, he sold or donated them.

I get that this is a bit extreme and raises all sorts of questions – like, what about seasonal things and that urn with your Nan's ashes? At the heart of this idea, however, is the fact that much of the stuff we have is superfluous and just adds complexity to our lives. Stuff has a weird stealthy ability to just creep into our homes and lives, and it fills up space and saps our energy without us even realising. Whether you do a full-on packing party, or just pack up some stuff you think you don't need and put it out of sight to see if you miss it – it's the same idea.

Based on my experience, as long as you never open the box again, you'll never miss a thing.

The verdict

Minimalism is a great philosophy, just remember that there's no universal number of things you should have – it's personal, *just make sure it's intentional.*

Our attachment to things can be complex; it can be challenging to go through the process of getting rid of them. I've found the process changes depending on what you're dealing with – *a set of sheets is different to a piece of your grandmother's china.* In each of the following chapters, I talk about how I tackle those items in more detail.

Step Two: What stuff comes in

By being intentional about what I purchase, I have a whole lot less stuff coming into my home and my life. This has had a massive impact. It's hard to quantify, but my 'back of an envelope' estimation is that, so far, I've saved more than NZ$10,000 and at least four working weeks of time. *Next time you pop to the shops to buy something, time yourself. It's terrifying.*

> ⊘ **TIME HACK** Shopping is a time warp. Buying less and skipping the shops has been, without question, the biggest time saving I've made.

When things do come in, I focus on making better choices about where they're coming from, what they're made of, how long they'll last and where they're going to end up. This all sounds way more complex than it actually is. It's now a super-quick subconscious process I run through, any time I need something.

Make do

Having a mindset of less means that I'll often figure out how to make do with something I already have. I'm constantly surprised at how I can find solutions that don't involve buying something.

Avoid temptation

Temptation is real. When I see nice things, I want them, I want that hit of instant gratification (although I'm not so keen on the feeling of buyer's remorse that comes afterwards).

I've learned that a simple thing is to avoid temptation.
- I don't spend my weekends browsing at malls.
- I've unsubscribed from online databases, so I'm not constantly bombarded with endless new bench-top appliances and end-of-season sales.
- I don't buy things on first sight – I'll take a micropause, or even sleep on it, or place items in an online shopping cart and leave them there for a few days, and see if I still want it in the morning. I never do.
- I believe in delayed gratification – the even-better hit you get when you have to wait for something you really want. (Remember that feeling from childhood?)

A story about temptation

I know a 'plant lady' (no, that's not a euphemism). Thankfully, she lives in another town, otherwise things would get a bit out of control. After one weekend visit, I came home with a new instalment of houseplants and needed pots to put them in.

So, I went to Kmart. That may not sound like a big deal for you, but it was for me (and for my kids). As an aspiring minimalist, I believe the world has enough stuff. But when I arrived at Kmart, ohhhhhhh – there was so much pretty stuff, and it was so cheap. How I wanted that stuff.

My then-five-year-old daughter looked like she'd uncovered some massive secret I'd been hiding from her (I kind of had been) – she now wanted all that stuff, too.

The temptation was immense. It was her incessant nagging for stuff that broke my trance. We left and went to the park.

After that experience, I discovered that the dark side of the force is strong and, for me, the best and easiest thing is to avoid temptation.

I found some second-hand pots on a local buy, sell and exchange page. Job done.

SUNSHINE FAIRY My daughter came home one day declaring that she needed a 'sunshine fairy' costume for pre-school the next day. My challenge to her was that we could use anything as long as it came from our home or garden. Sticks, dental floss (compostable, of course), scarves and a leaf garland made her the best damn sunshine fairy I've ever seen. It was also really fun to do together. And before you write it off for taking too long, it took us 20 minutes, which is less time than it would have taken for us to drive to the dollar store up the road.

Borrow and share

These days, it seems, it's all about individual ownership. Our houses have become cookie-cutter storage boxes for all the same stuff. Lift the roofs off a group of houses in a typical suburban cluster and you'd spot a similar pattern of ownership and see all the items that are hardly ever used.

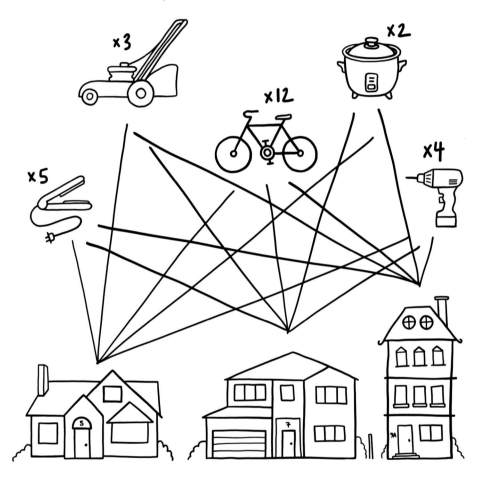

I even remember seeing them given away as part of a real estate deal. Buy a house, get a drill!

Think of the humble power drill. Almost every household I know owns one. And I get why – they're now super affordable, it's handy to have your own, and the sound of using it sends ripples of testosterone (or female empowerment) through suburban streets. It's almost a rite of passage.

But here's the rub … it's estimated that the average power drill will only be used for 12 to 15 minutes in its lifetime – just 12 to 15 minutes! In her TEDx talk, 'The case for collaborative consumption', Rachel Botsman said, 'What you need is the hole, not the drill.' It's so obvious when you think about it. As she says, we need access over ownership. Her case looks at the 'idling capacity' of things – the fact that 99.9% of the time, that drill of ours is just sitting there.

Collaborative consumption, or the sharing economy, taps into that.

While we've always had book libraries, there's a resurgence of libraries for things like tools, toys and clothing. Technology is enabling sharing at scale with websites such as Airbnb, and car sharing. (I don't know if Tinder should make the list?) The sharing economy allows us to access things with less impact.

You can also just keep it low key, and borrow or share things with people you know. We own very few tools; instead, we hire or borrow them from mates and neighbours. It's not about being those tight-arses who don't want to buy their own – we take care of their tools and trade our time, dinner or something else tangible in return.

Fix things

Sometimes, stuff breaks and sometimes, it feels like the easiest thing to do is to buy a new one. My default is now to see if I (or someone else) can fix it first.

Planned obsolescence and a decline in repair services mean it can be tricky, or expensive, to find the parts or skills needed to repair things. I've had more than one repairperson give me that weird look when I've said I would rather repair over replace, despite the cost being similar. I do it because it's important to me to do my part in creating demand for a repair mentality – but I totally get that it might not be seen as the most rational thing to do!

I don't know what I'd do without cable ties and a good tube of glue.

> **REPAIR CAFÉS** There is an exciting movement happening – repair cafés. Clever people volunteer their time to help people fix their things. From hemming pants to fixing vacuum cleaners to resoldering jewellery, it's about making things last as well as passing on the skills needed for people to do it themselves. Search for a repair café in your area, or even start your own – they're a bloody great fundraising idea, just saying.

How I buy

Where to shop

In the past five years, I've changed where I shop – I've barely set foot in a shopping mall. I'm a huge fan of buying second-hand; the stuff already exists and, if I can keep it in use, it's a good thing. I remember when you had to trawl the classifieds section of the local newspaper, or get up early to get to a garage sale. Technology means we now have so much choice at our fingertips. I also have my favourite local op shops, where they always have an amazing selection. Supporting a charity also has the feel-good factor.

Is it more time consuming? Ahh, no. Often, I can find what I need from the comfort of my couch and, even if I do have to hunt for something a bit harder, the fact that I'm buying so much less overall means I'm still way better off in the time stakes.

> ⊘ **TIME HACK** I keep a list of things I need, or need to replace, on my phone. Then when I hit the op shops, I'll keep an eye out for things on the list.

Buying new

Like Neil, my cast-iron frying pan – that guy is going to outlive all of us. You will never regret buying quality.

When I go all out and buy something new, I'll always try to buy from companies that are being environmentally responsible and will opt for quality that lasts. I get that, sometimes, this can feel uncomfortable because it's going to have a higher initial outlay, but Accounting 101 (or was it Mum?) taught me that I should look at the total lifetime cost. Buying less also means that better quality is more affordable.

I also consider:

- What it's made from (and what will happen to it at the end of its useful life)?
- How is it made/manufactured (and what's the impact)?
- Who made it? (I love supporting independent makers.)
- Where has it come from (how far has it had to travel)?
- How is it packaged?

Don't worry, this doesn't include necessities such as food!

I don't want you to tie yourself up in knots, trying to find the perfect solution. If you consider any of these questions and make a better choice, then it's a win. Imperfect action, people!

⊘ **TIME HACK** Get amongst 'Buy nothing new October', or pick your own month and challenge yourself – you'll save a heap of time 'not' shopping.

Step Three: Letting things go

When I'm ready to let still-useful things go, I'm mindful of where they're going. I see this as the final part of the whole journey of valuing our things. I also get a buzz knowing that my things are going somewhere where they will be valued and used by others.

Re-homing

Our group of friends has a carousel of kids' clothes that does the rounds – I love seeing my mates' kids in clothes that my own kids have outgrown.

Charity shops

Before doing a drop-off, I have a conversation with my local charity shops to see what things they need and what sells well.

Man, these guys do such an epic job of reducing waste and supporting our communities. My golden rule is to only donate things I think other people would be willing to buy. If clothes or homewares are broken, stained or have generally had it, charity shops won't be able to sell them – it's just a case of being honest and not passing the buck.

Other charities

There are also charities that accept specific things and get them into the right hands: a lot of women's charities need good-quality baby gear; Dress for Success provides professional clothing to women to help them achieve economic independence; Uplift Bras provides bras to women who otherwise wouldn't be able to access them; and Lazy Sneakers collects sneakers and distributes to people who need them.

FINDING HOMES Use the power of social media to find charities and other organisations looking for specific items. Check out Facebook waste forums like Zero Waste in NZ! or Zero Waste Australia.

Sell stuff

The power of the World Wide Web means that it's easier than ever to find buyers who genuinely want your stuff. Pages such as Trade Me, Gumtree and eBay all can help you re-home things.

In my initial purge of stuff, I sold lots on Trade Me and made over $4k, which paid for a holiday – boom!

⊘ **TIME HACK** If you can't find the time to list items for sale, outsource it to someone who needs a bit of pocket money.

Pay it Forward

Thanks to social media, there's a heap of local Pay It Forward pages out there, or check out freecycle.org, where you can list things free to a good home. I've been amazed at things that people want – from jars to old CDs, and trees that have been dug out of a garden.

Toy libraries

I've passed on some good-quality toys to our local toy library. The kids have even borrowed those toys a few times – such a cool way to teach them about sharing things. → For more on toy libraries, see page 193.

Making the change

Changing our relationship with stuff has been a major breakthrough in simplifying our lives. Shifting our mindset to reconnect with the value of what we own, and to stop the constant quest for more, has saved us so much time, money and energy, and it's been weirdly freeing.

In the next few chapters, I'll share more detail about what we've done and how we've achieved it.

BUSY TIPS – WHERE TO START?

- Unsubscribe from marketing emails to avoid being tempted by all the shiny things.
- Sign up for a 30-day minimalism challenge or 'Buy nothing new October'.
- Next time you feel like you need to shoot to the shop to buy something, see if there's a way you can make do with something you already have.
- Gather up that pile of broken things and head off to a repair café.

AT HOME

'Have nothing in your house that you do not know to be useful, or believe to be beautiful.' – **WILLIAM MORRIS**

When we bought our home, my goal was for a place where I only had to plug in my vacuum cleaner once to reach every room. While I'm not a huge fan of vacuuming, there was obviously way more to the decision than just that.

Choosing a smaller house was symbolic of the life we wanted to lead. As a family, we want to live with less stuff, less waste and less impact – with more simplicity and more time. This mindset now drives the big life choices we make. Getting out of the big city and going smaller with our house was a massive turning point; it's kind of reverse-engineered our life so that it fits with our priorities.

I've been blown away by how dramatic the upsides are from going smaller.

The upsides of living smaller

Saving time

Having everything on a smaller scale saves time. Previously, we were living in a four-bedroom two-bathroom home – I've figured out that, compared to now, I was spending an extra 32 minutes on my weekly cleaning (yep, I measure these things). That's an additional 28 hours, or 3.5 workdays per year! And that's not even taking into account the extra window cleaning (if you're into that). Combine this figure with other home maintenance tasks, looking for things, opening/closing extra curtains – I know it sounds ridiculous, but this stuff fascinates me. When you add it all up, it's far from insignificant. There are so many other things I would rather be doing with that time.

> ⊘ **TIME HACK** Smaller house = less time cleaning, maintaining and searching for things.

Saving money

Smaller is cheaper – it's simple economics.

- Lower purchase cost for a smaller house
- Buying less furniture, artwork, doilies and fewer appliances and other stuff
- Less on heating and electricity
- Less maintenance – things like painting, repairs and re-carpeting are on a smaller scale
- Lower property rates

Saving money and breaking up with the constant quest for more has given us more freedom of choice. Both my husband and I have been able to break up with our corporate salaries. We've both reinvented the way we work – we're now working fewer hours and in jobs that are way more aligned with our purpose.

Consuming less

Living smaller has meant we've decreased our impact without even thinking about it. We live to the space we have, which means we're consuming way less. Think fewer cleaning products, furniture, linen, ditties (that's what my husband calls knick-knacks and artwork), carpet, appliances … which means less stuff ultimately ending up in landfill. We also consume less of other resources such as electricity and water – we're not heating or servicing areas of our home that we're not using.

THE MINDSET

The physical act of going smaller was relatively easy, but I had to make sure my mindset was also along for the ride.

Breaking up with more

Our society is wired to be on a constant quest for more. When it comes to our homes and our stuff, it's often about newer, bigger and better. Australia and New Zealand have some of the world's largest square-metre houses per person – huge has become the norm.

I've consciously had to break up with the drive for wanting bigger and newer – it was pretty ingrained. I often feel like our family is swimming against the tide and, occasionally, I worry about other people's expectations. But then I remember that everything in life is a choice and we're making the right one for us.

A story about choice

We have friends with big houses. Sometimes, after visiting, my kids will ask, 'Why can't we have a big house, like Nigella?' (Not her real name.) 'Why can't we have a playroom, swimming pool, mudroom and portico?' (I love that word.)

I'm not going to lie – I often ask myself the same question. I still compare myself to other people – I'm only human. Sometimes, I still want the stuff that other people have. Having to explain things to my kids helps me to get things straight in my own head as well.

Here's what we talk about: everything in life is a choice – we all have limited time, energy and resources, and we need to choose how to spend them.

As a family, we choose to have a smaller low-maintenance house without much stuff. Making this choice means we have more freedom to do other things that are important to our family. We work less, go on more holidays, and have more time to just hang out.

If I ever need perspective, I remind myself that it takes me only 45 minutes to clean my whole house. I'm sold.

Make it work

I have a friend who is building a new house. Her mother was shocked to hear they weren't putting in a guest toilet. Her concern was that, with my friend's two young boys using the toilet, it wouldn't be up to scratch for visitors.

Don't get me wrong, I totally appreciate the messy interactions that happen when boys and toilets meet – but if you were to do the usage analysis, a guest toilet would probably sit unused 99.25%* of the time (*totally made up, but it would be most of the time). As my friend said, why should I build an extra room when I can solve it by helping my boys learn to keep the toilet clean? (A great life skill that will be appreciated by many.)

Similarly, we don't have a spare room, we just have the kids share a room for the few nights a year when people come to stay. The one time we had a mass onslaught of friends, we found an Airbnb just around the corner.

Our house suits our needs for the vast majority of the time, and we figure out what to do for the handful of times it doesn't.

Bringing families closer together

Living smaller means that we're physically closer together. I get that this is a double-edged sword! Maybe it will change as my kids get older but, in the meantime, I actually quite like my family and enjoy having conversations and interacting with what they're doing when we're at home together. As long as everyone has their own space to escape to, then it works for us.

GETTING IT DONE

Make the most of your space

Live to the space

We have a small lounge. Instead of trying to squeeze all our furniture into it, we got rid of some. This makes the space way more usable. It's a compact space but there's always more than enough room for the kids to build huts, my erratic, impromptu yoga sessions and floor picnics. We also have a family rule that you have to put away what you're using before getting anything else out.

> ⊘ **TIME HACK** Packing up straight away is a necessity with small spaces, but it's also an awesome habit for everyone.

Apart from the random pile of papers, phone chargers and pens on a corner of the kitchen bench.

I love the idea of multifunctional spaces. One day, I'd love to have one of those beds that folds into the wall (*I'm sure I got the idea from watching 'Full House' as a child*), or switch to Japanese futons that you pack away. It's such a smart idea – beds just sit there all day, taking up space!

Everything in its place

Having less of everything makes it easier to have a place for everything and frees up usable space.

I'm pretty intentional about where stuff goes in our home – this keeps me sane and frees up the space so it's usable.

Having less stuff means I've always got more than enough cupboard space for everything. I'm also a big fan of Marie Kondo's box approach. I'm not patient enough to keep all small things orderly, and having boxes means I can get away with throwing items in while keeping everything together and easy to find.

> ⊘ **TIME HACK** I keep kids' art supplies stored in large lidded containers, kitchen utensils separated in shoe box lids and school bags hung on hooks inside the hall cupboard.

While good storage and organisation are important, be wary of using this as an excuse to just have more stuff!

Both my kids have drawstring
bags for all of their toys.
It means they can always
see everything they have and
makes packing up super easy.

CASE STUDY: SMALLER AND SIMPLER

I love chatting with my friend Carl – together with wife Jo and two boys, their family is always coming up with new ways to make their lives simpler.

Carl's accountant recently told him that Carl is the first client he's had who is focused on increasing time instead of money.

The small shed

Carl chose a small 4 x 2.3 m shed intentionally, which is both the garage and the whole family's storage space. Instead of getting better at stacking stuff, every year the family pulls everything out and makes sure only the priority things (which they're actually using) make the cut.

The 20-min mow

Embracing his love of golf courses, Carl has dedicated some areas as 'rough' to save time on mowing.

And don't get me started on the campervan that Carl fitted out. They hit the road in it for six weeks over summer.

This is Carl and his small shed!

'Rough' areas to save time mowing

Bella

Less stuff in your space

Household stuff

If you had opened my linen cupboard a few years ago, you would have found enough sheets to sleep 18 people (with both summer and winter options).

We live in a 110 square metre house – I'm pretty sure I couldn't actually fit that many people on my floor. Then there's the fact that it would never happen. It was a case of only ever using the first few sets on the top of the pile and never getting to the other ones (the classic 80/20 rule). I now have two summer sets and one winter set per bed.

If I have a massive influx of friends wanting to stay, I can rock out the sleeping bags or ask them to bring their own sheets.

I figured out I had all that linen 'just in case'. Statistically, that 'just in case' was highly unlikely to ever happen. I realised that, if it did, I had ways of dealing with it.

It wasn't only the sheets. Our home was full of things we rarely used. It felt like the amount of stuff we owned was constantly multiplying. All of it was taking up space, time and energy, and holding onto it, when other people could be using it, started to feel like a waste.

> **'JUST IN CASE'** We feel like we need certain things. We have things 'just in case' (like my linen stash), or maybe we were given them as a wedding present, or maybe Target or Briscoes had a sale. Sometimes, we hold onto things because they have meaning, or because we're conditioned to feel like we should own things. By shifting to being conscious of why you're holding onto things, you can address whether or not you really need them.

In the winter, if a flannelette set isn't dry in time, I just roll with summer ones. Once during a tummy bug, I ran out of dry single sheets so just doubled over the big ones.

Furniture

F-waste is a thing. Yep, we're wasting so much furniture at home and work, it needs its own abbreviation.

A generation ago, furniture and décor was an investment that you pretty much had for life. Now, it's a fashion trend with seasonal colours, textures and designs. At the risk of sounding like my grandfather – things also just aren't made to last like they used to.

I'm a big fan of second-hand furniture. It has a bit of personality and you get a good sense of how it lasts and looks after a bit of wear and tear. I'd way rather get something restored and re-covered than buy it new.

I aim for timeless design that's not going to date. I don't have a crystal ball, but I've been into Scandinavian design for a while – it's functional, intentional and beautiful, and it hasn't gone out of style yet (at least, I don't think it has).

Also, I consciously don't flip through furniture catalogues or read home and garden magazines – if I don't look, I don't know what I'm missing. It's not that I don't take pride in how my home looks; I just know what I like – I'm backing myself – and it's about not following fashion whims.

⊘ **TIME HACK** Backing your own style and avoiding temptation means you spend less time browsing, and buying things you don't need.

MULTIFUNCTIONED DESIGN

I'm in awe of a well-designed tiny house or campervan – it's like they've been designed by the makers of Transformers. Furniture and fittings fold out, expand and convert to everything you need.

I'm not alone either – IKEA has recently announced a partnership with a robotics company – yep, robotic furniture that can transform and fold away. The Jetsons is totally coming true.

While I'm not quite at the point of robotics, I have a dose of that mentality when I need to make furniture decisions. Having trundle beds gives us twice the bed in the same amount of space, and I love our expandable dining-room table.

Décor

My décor of choice is plants. Plants never go out of style and they earn a ton of bonus points for cleaning the air, too. I started getting into houseplants when my friend told me I'd taken the minimalism thing too far, and my house looked weirdly empty and stark. My mission has been to find plants that are low maintenance, make my home healthier and look good!

Research shows that people living with plants are happier and healthier.

NIC-APPROVED HOUSEPLANTS

Here's my list of favourite houseplants:
- Snake plant
- Peace lily
- Monstera, common name Fruit salad/Swiss cheese plant (or the 'huge one in the corner' as it's called at our place)
- String of pearls (I have a three-week reminder in my phone to water it)
- Heart leaf philodendron (this loves to climb everywhere)
- Fiddle leaf fig
- Devil's ivy

⊘ **TIME HACK** Plants look awesome, clean the air and keep multiplying, so I can share the love by giving away their plant babies as gifts!

Surgical tape held this kettle together for a long time. I now have a stovetop one which should outlast me.

Peace Lily

Kitchen appliances

When it comes to kitchen appliances, I'm pretty ruthless. If we don't use them regularly, then we don't have them.

Making do

There's normally a way around things – if I feel the whim to make my own bread a couple of times a year, then I make it by hand. Instead of a separate spice grinder, I just throw everything into the blender. We've also got rid of our toasted sandwich maker and just use the frying pan.

Sourcing

If I'm ever tempted to buy a new kitchen appliance, I'll ask around and see if I can borrow one first. Most of the time, I'll use it a couple of times before the novelty wears off, or I find it's really niggly to clean or doesn't quite do what I want it to. I'm clearly not the only one – every time I go into a charity shop, I'm guaranteed to spot at least two yoghurt-makers, a bread-maker and a popcorn machine.

If I trial an appliance and decide it's something that I'll use a lot, then they're normally easy to find second-hand.

> ⊘ **TIME HACK** Fewer appliances, fewer things
> to clean and clutter up the cupboards.

Sentimental items

I highly recommend that you get a few wins under your belt before you start trying to reduce your sentimental items! This is better tackled once you're in the swing of things.

Memories don't live in objects; they live in your mind. Imagine that Aunt Vera owned an antique vase, which she passed on to her niece Nancy. Nancy loves it dearly because it evokes memories of her childhood. When she moves into a retirement village, she passes it on to her son Steve. He holds onto it because his mum told him to, so he keeps it in the hall cupboard – his wife, Judy, doesn't like it. He then downsizes and passes it on to daughter Sarah, telling her she has to keep this vase because it belonged to Great-Great-Aunt Vera, who she's never met. Sarah puts it in a storage unit.

Aunt Vera's vase – memories live in us, not in objects.

Aunt Vera was probably an awesome human, and maybe she saved the money she earned from her first job as a seamstress in London and bought the vase from the Portobello markets, where she met and fell in love with her husband, Robert. We have the vase, but we've lost the memory.

We grant a lot of power to objects, whereas the power is really in the memories and stories that make us human.

Holding onto things out of obligation, storing them in a cupboard and then passing them on doesn't keep memories alive. Stories do.

Should it stay or should it go?

- Less doesn't mean none! Having fewer things means you can value and appreciate them more.
- Write down family memories and stories in a book that can be passed on – you can even take photos of the objects and include them in the book. I'd love to pass on a book of family stories to my kids, instead of a shipping container full of stuff.

> ⊘ **TIME HACK** If someone in your family loves writing, ask them to capture some memories, and do something for them in exchange.

- Use your things, or choose a few of your favourites to have on display, instead of hiding them in the cupboard.
- Find someone who can use it – I love knowing that my old possessions are out there, being loved and used. You can even write down the story of the object and pass it on to the new owner.
- If you think getting rid of something is going to really upset someone, start by having the conversation. You might be surprised.

PRIZED POSSESSIONS

Here's my inventory of sentimental items:

- One shoebox of letters, old diaries, books, school reports, tickets and photos.
- Some photos are on display and we have a couple of physical photo albums. The rest are digital.
- The baby blanket my grandmother knitted for my brother, which I also used with my kids.
- Two necklaces that I wear regularly.
- Squeaky, my childhood doll
- The stone from my grandmother's engagement ring is in my wedding ring. I had the band melted down and turned into earrings for my mum – I was never going to wear it as it was.
- The kids use the Bunnykins plates that I used when I was a child.
- Frames on the wall contain wedding photos and baby thank-you cards from friends (anyone who walks into our house can't help but look at them).
- One day, I'll inherit a LOT of china ... Don't worry, Mum, I'll figure something out.

Lots of minimalists talk about scanning old documents and going fully digital, but I find there's still nothing like holding them in your hand so I'm not quite at that point yet ...

TRIBUTE PHOTO ALBUM My friend Tori had the ingenious idea of taking annual photos of her kids with their favourite possessions. She now doesn't need to hang on to all that stuff – she can hang the pictures on the wall to keep those memories alive.

CASE STUDY: EMMA'S JOURNEY

I met Emma when she came on one of my house tours. She was back in town to sort through the family home after her mum had passed away. We talked about how she'd found ways to let go of things and how this had changed her relationship with the stuff in her own life.

A large part of Emma's journey has been about redefining the value of things. For her, value is not about money, but about emotional connection. It's about having and holding onto things that evoke happy memories and that make her feel good. It's also about having just the right number of things, so she can appreciate and connect with them every day, instead of hiding them away in a cupboard.

When it came to letting go of the rest of her mum's stuff, here are a few things that helped:

- If she knew her mum's things could be valued by others, it was easier to let them go. Emma found charities and organisations that had a connection with the family and could use the goods.
- Emma is a writer – she took the time to journal many of the memories that came up as she sorted through things with her siblings. She loved how this gave their memories permanence and made it easier to let go of items.

Tools

We pay someone to mow our lawns. There, I said it! It's something my embedded work ethic still struggles with coming clean about. We started outsourcing the mowing when we were renting, because we didn't own a lawnmower and were still pretty transient. Then I started on this journey and didn't want more stuff in the garage.

I'm sure I could approach our neighbour about borrowing his, but I love the time-saving aspect of not having to think about it. I'd also feel stink taking the business off Stephen, who has been doing our lawns for years. It's his livelihood and he's good at it.

We have some basic tools to do stuff around the house. Most of them were hand-me-downs, or we've bought them from the local charity shop.

We tend to have a working-bee type approach where, a couple of times a year, we'll spend the whole weekend in the garden or doing maintenance. We'll then borrow (normally in exchange for dinner) or hire the things we need. This gives us a deadline and means we work our arses off to get it done.

> ⊘ **TIME HACK** Check to see if there's a tool library in your area – they're popping up all over the place and are a great way to get your hands on all sorts of helpful items.

FYI, our mower would be idle for about 8,723 hours per year, or 99.85% of the time.

I know people who mow their neighbour's lawn in exchange for fresh produce out of the garden.

Borrow and return me

Sports gear

Use it or lose it

I'd love to know the statistic for how many unused Ab Blasters there are sitting in garages globally, or how many home treadmills are being used as clothes-drying racks. It'd be great to have rock-hard abs in just minutes a day and fit in my morning jog as I lovingly watch my children eat breakfast – but alas, my life is not an infomercial!

If you're tempted by gym gear, try renting or borrowing it first (I bet you'll be able to find an unused Ab Blaster in a matter of two conversations = 2 degrees of Ab Blaster separation). Otherwise, if you can make it to the gym, give that a go first and see if it sticks.

If you play a sport or have a hobby that needs gear and you're using it, then embrace it. But if you've got stuff sitting around gathering dust, then it might be worth reviewing.

I've had to work through my previous-life hobby stuff. I used to snowboard (sort of) and I kept holding onto the gear for when I got back into it. After not setting foot on a ski field for eight years, it was time to let it go. Sure, there's a chance I might take it up again one day but, by that time, all my gear would be well out of fashion or moth eaten or mouldy (in the meantime, it could be being used by someone else). If I do happen to hit the slopes again, there's no shortage of rental options to tap into.

I'm not saying to get rid of things if you're legit going to use them – just be honest with yourself.

Renovating or building

Most estimates put waste from the construction and demolition industry at between a third and a half of the total waste in Australia and NZ. It's a big deal!

If you're looking at building or renovating, have the conversation with your potential builder or supplier at the outset.

We were pulling down our old shed. When talking to demolition providers, I asked what they did with the waste. On my fourth call, I found someone who was prepared to separate the materials and reuse or recycle it. They got the job.

When we were replacing some windows, I had the same conversation. The guys who sent the old glass to be crushed and used for swimming pool filtration were the ones who got the job.

Of course, they also had to be providing a good product and service at a competitive price, but if they're being mindful of their total impact, it's a proven indication of a company that gives a sh!t.

I make sure to give them feedback that reducing their waste was a deciding factor for me.

> ⊘ **TIME HACK** A simple upfront conversation can be all it takes to make better choices. Even if change doesn't happen straight away, you've helped seed the idea.

Electronics

My old Nokia 3310 and I went through some good times together. I used that mobile phone for at least five years and still nothing compares to its battery life. These days, the speed of technology innovation is eye-watering. No sooner do you upgrade and the next model, plus version or facial recognition ability (life has actually become Minority Report) is on the shelf. You can shun the desire to update but, eventually, planned obsolescence will get ya – things won't be compatible, supported or you can't get parts for it. Whether it's our fridge, laptop, printer or kids' toys, the speed at which we're buying and throwing out our electronics (e-waste) is frightening.

Throwing e-waste in a landfill is also problematic, due to the materials and the risk of battery fires. Some places are now even banning it from landfill. So, how do we navigate electronics when they've become such a fundamental part of our modern-day lives?

The Global E-waste Monitor 2017 report found that, in Australia and NZ, we're creating around 20 kg e-waste per person per year, and it's increasing really fast.

Buy less

It's not rocket science, but the best thing we can do is make things last.

- We only replace things when they need replacing.
- I'll protect the living daylights out of my phones and laptops, with screen protectors and bounce-proof cases, as soon as I get them.
- If electronics break, I'll try to get them fixed. Sometimes it sucks because it's almost cheaper to replace them (like the element on my stove recently), but it's important to me to support the demand for repairs.

DON'T UPGRADE AS OFTEN Comment from Mike: I'm a technology guy, and I used to always need the latest version of everything. I still like good stuff, but I've slowed down how frequently I upgrade. Avoiding temptation has been a massive help – I don't go browsing in the shops or online like I used to.

⊘ **TIME HACK** Getting good-quality cases and screen protectors will save you having to replace and repair your electronics as often. Two smashed phone screens in 3 weeks taught me this!

Sourcing products

I'll always ask the manufacturers if they offer refurbished models. This means I can get second-hand items but still be covered by a warranty. We've sourced all our laptops this way – it's saved us a heap of money and they've been like new.

It's a good idea to ask about the repair services available if you're making a large purchase.

End of the line

When you're done with electronic gear, it feels good to be able to pass it on if it's still working. Hand-me-down electronics are great, or if you're donating them, just check if your charity shop has the ability to test electronics, otherwise they probably can't accept them.

Even if your products are no longer working, it's useful to offer them on the likes of Pay It Forward pages, because some people might be able to fix them or use them for parts.

⊘ **TIME HACK** Posting available items online may mean you don't even need to leave the house – people will come to you to collect them.

If your electronics are at the point of recycling, check with your local council to learn about e-waste recycling in your area. E-waste recyclers will dismantle things and recycle components where possible.

@ **FIND IT ONLINE** When it comes to mobile phones, there are various take-back schemes available free of charge, and some even benefit local charities. Check out mobilemuster.com.au and remobile.org.nz.

⊘ **TIME HACK** Invest in rechargeable batteries for your electronics and you'll never need to buy them again – and you'll skip all the e-waste.

PRODUCT STEWARDSHIP

Product stewardship means taking responsibility for reducing a product's environmental impact. From furniture and electronics to paint and car tyres, it can occur on any product and anywhere in the chain, from the producer to the brand-owner, importer, retailer or consumer. Schemes exist all over the world – not only do they make sense, they also work.

Here's how it can go:

- You buy a new TV, and included in the purchase price is an extra $10.
- This $10 is put into an industry-wide fund, which builds a facility and distribution network to collect and process old TVs.
- When your old TV stops working, you go and buy a new one, and return the old one to the store.
- The old one gets sent to the recycling facility and is either refurbished and reused, or the materials are reused to make new TVs.

I'm all for supporting product stewardship because it's about environmental responsibility and we need more of that. If I ever have the chance to sign a petition or support a product stewardship initiative, then I'm up for it.

BUSY TIPS – WHERE TO START?

- Gather up your stash of broken things and get along to a repair café.
- Sign up for a 30-day minimalism challenge with a friend, and then offer unwanted items to others.
- Select tradies who reuse or recycle materials whenever possible and dispose of rubbish responsibly.
- Unsubscribe from that homeware catalogue.

FASHION

'Buy less, choose well, make it last.' **– VIVIENNE WESTWOOD**

The year was 1992. I was consumed with desire for a pair of Levi's 501 jeans. Because I was 14 years old and earning NZ$4.60 an hour in my part-time job, it took me months to save the NZ$120 I needed for them to be mine.

I vividly remember the anticipation and subsequent joy I got from buying them – the hit of delayed gratification was so good! Quarter of a century later, I can honestly say it was a teenage life event. Man, I loved those jeans, and I wore them to within an inappropriate inch of their life.

Alas, those heady 501 days are now just a nostalgic memory – the way we value our clothes isn't quite what it used to be.

I once sat next to a guy at a conference – I think his name was Dave. He told me that his dad had always worked in the women's clothing industry. Dave's dad had recounted a time, back in the '70s, when his company was doing trend forecasting. They projected that, one day, disposable clothing would be a thing. Humans would wear things once, then throw them away. It might have felt a bit sci-fi at the time but, it turns out, we're not that far off it.

We're buying more clothing than ever before and disposing of it at a freaken astounding rate! The irony is that, instead of making our lives easier, we're just spending way more time shopping and getting frustrated by our crammed wardrobes.

The hidden cost of fast fashion

The Ellen MacArthur foundation states that, in the last 15 years, the amount of clothing being manufactured has doubled.

Fondly referred to as 'fast fashion' – a good chunk of the industry is all about buying more clothes, more often, for less money. No longer are there just the two seasons: warm and cold. Many clothing retailers have numerous collections each year, with some refreshing them weekly. The speed and scale of production now means that, mere days after a Kardashian wears a new style, it's available on the High Street store racks – all at a very affordable price.

Clothes are cheaper, shops are more accessible and we're spoiled for choice. We can keep up with the latest micro-trends and fill our wardrobes to bulging. It's too easy to fuel that hit of instant gratification from buying new things.

I get it. It feels good to roll up to work or a function, rocking a new get-up … but there's a heap of impact in the choices we make.

THE MINDSET

The good news is that sustainable fashion doesn't mean we all have to start wearing handcrafted beige macramé muumuus year-round – unless that's what you're into. You don't need to give up on fashion or let yourself go.

What we wear is a key way that we express ourselves – no matter where you are on the fashion spectrum. Decreasing our impact is about embracing that self-expression, then finding ways to make better, more conscious, choices that suit us. For me, the shift has come in reconnecting with the value of what I wear.

What follows are some of the changes I've made when it comes to my wardrobe. Consistent with the rest of my mission, I'm all about reducing my impact, all while making my life simpler by saving time and money. And there are no macramé muumuus in sight.

FASHION STATS TO BLOW YOUR MIND

One rubbish truck-full of clothes is burned or sent to landfill every second! This is enough to fill Sydney Harbour every year.

It is estimated that clothes release 500,000 tonnes of microfibres into the ocean every year – equivalent to more than 50 billion plastic bottles.

Total greenhouse gas emissions from textiles production are more than all international flights and maritime shipping combined.

 VS.

Each year, up to 16% of the world's pesticides are used in cotton farming. The chemicals degrade soil and pollute water, as well as impacting the health of farmers and pickers.

Source: Ellen MacArthur Foundation

GETTING IT DONE

Have fewer clothes

When I started reading about reducing my wardrobe, I got a bit sick of people raving about how much easier it made life and how much time they'd saved. My bullsh!t bell was ringing hard. How much time and energy do we really spend choosing what to wear each day?

It's estimated that we regularly wear only 20–30% of the stuff we have in our wardrobes. This is the stuff that you feel good in – you know, the favourites you keep coming back to. The rest of it is kinda just noise – that stuff you sift through to get to those favourites. The things you try on in the midst of your time-poor morning routine then throw into a pile on the floor because it doesn't quite fit or just doesn't sit right, the colour doesn't really suit you, or it adds unnecessary volume to your hips.

I totally underestimated the effect of all that other wardrobe 'noise'. My bullsh!t bell was finally silenced as I realised that simplifying my wardrobe was a game changer. It was easier to find clothes and keep them tidy, it cut down on decision fatigue, and my washing pile shrank. Having less, and loving what I have, also means I can get my head around looking after my things better – I'll hang clothes properly and get items repaired, altered or resoled.

I have also become like those people in the magazines, who wear nine pieces in 52 ways … Well, not quite, but I've been surprised at my own creativity when it comes to putting what I have together in different outfit combinations.

Then there are the times that I need to pack to go away. Oh, my word, do I love having less then! I know that anything I pack will be a good choice because I feel good in everything I have – I'm almost at the point of being able to pack everything I own without even filling my suitcase. So. Easy.

Getting to less

To get rid of the 80% of stuff that I wasn't wearing, I spent two hours of my life trying everything on and being really honest about whether or not I felt good in it. I did pack up a cheeky pile of items that I wasn't quite ready to let go and stashed them in the spare room – but two months later, I couldn't even remember what was in the box and never missed a thing.

It's now just a rolling process. If I don't wear something for ages, or try it on and take it off straight away because it doesn't feel good, I put it on the top shelf in my wardrobe to await its new home.

That's what worked for me, but people have come up with a heap of other techniques to help get you to the point of less. Find the approach, or the mix, that works for you.

I've had this blue top for more than 10 years. I always feel good in it and often wear it when I'm delivering speaking engagements. Instead of worrying about being judged for wearing the same thing, I've embraced the point it's proving: #bluetop

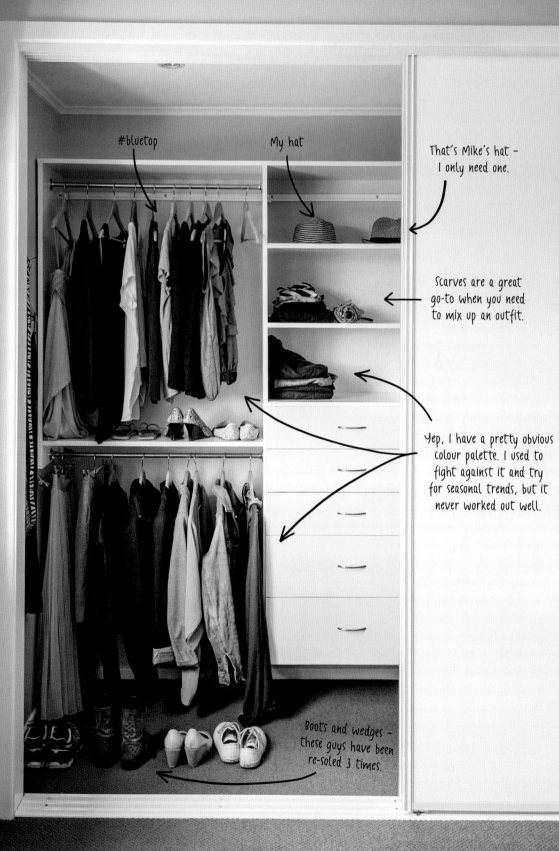

Marie Kondo's KonMari™ method

- Put all your clothes in a pile on your bed or the bedroom floor – yep, every single item, even the stuff in the washing pile.
- Pick up each item and ask yourself if it sparks joy in you. (aka: Do you love it?)
- No joy, no making the cut.
- For things that are hard to let go, thank them for their service. Yes, it felt ridiculous, but thanking my worn and tired high heels for all the good times we had together made it that much easier to set them free.

Project 333™

- This is an online challenge where you trial having only 33 items in your wardrobe for three months.
- Your 33 items include shoes, accessories, jewellery and outerwear.
- You get a free pass on exercise gear, underwear, sleepwear and at-home lounge wear. (I'm guessing they're referring to my Ugg boots and trackies.)
- Everything else gets boxed up and placed out of sight.
- After the 3 months is over, it's up to you what you do with the boxed items. The intent is that you've adjusted to living with fewer items and can donate, sell or give away the things you're not wearing. You may find there are some favourites you've missed or seasonal items you need to hang on to – and that's ok.

The reverse-hanger approach

- Turn all the clothes hangers in your wardrobe to face the same way.
- Each time you wear an item, return it to your wardrobe with the hanger facing the other way.
- At the end of a set period of time, get rid of anything that hasn't been turned around.

What comes in

Curate your wardrobe

Make conscious choices about what comes into your wardrobe. When it comes to fashion, there are lots of ways to make better choices – choose the priorities that best suit you. Here are how my priorities normally roll out.

1. Love it

I have to LOVE what comes into my wardrobe and be prepared to wear it a number of times. This means that a LOT less comes into my wardrobe.

I've got a pretty good sense of what suits me – I think. If you're not sure, hire a stylist, have your colours done or ask an extremely honest friend.

I avoid anything that's not my colour, cut or shape. I've got a thing about my knees, and I know that I will ALWAYS regret wearing something that shows them too much – I spent years fighting it, but now, I just embrace it. Being confident in my style means I can break up with the marketing pressures of following the latest trend (within reason, of course – I aim for timeless design as opposed to fleeting trends).

NIC'S TAKE ON THE CAPSULE WARDROBE

When I first heard the term 'capsule wardrobe', I imagined some space-aged pod-shaped cupboard housing lots of white clothes. I was wrong – a capsule wardrobe is actually a minimal wardrobe that is made up of a set number of versatile items that you can mix and match.

Flick to the fashion section of any women's magazine and you'll see the 'must haves' for the season, laid out capsule wardrobe-esque on a double-page spread.

There are a tonne of prescriptive lists out there detailing the items you need to compile your own versatile wardrobe. At the press of a 'buy now' button, you can even be sent a generic pre-assembled monochrome capsule wardrobe in your size!

I'm into the idea of a capsule wardrobe, because it makes you think about having versatile pieces that can be mixed and matched. It also makes you consider owning less stuff – that is, unless you go out and buy a new capsule wardrobe every season!

For some people, having a specific number and prescriptive list of items might be what they need to get the ball rolling. But for me, it's about working to my own number and my own style. I just did a quick browse of online recommendations for capsule wardrobes; the first one included a cropped T-shirt as a key item. Umm ... yeah, not since the '80s has that been a good idea for me!

The verdict

I see capsule wardrobes as a good philosophy. They can be great inspiration, but don't get tied up in the detail if it's not working for you.

Opposite is my version of a 'capsule wardrobe' and roughly what I have most of the time.

I aim to go for things that can be dressed up or down and will go for neutral colours – especially on the bottom half.

General

7 pairs of underwear (a hangover from having days
    of the week undies when I was a child)
4 bras (2 black, 1 white, 1 strapless)
2 cotton singlets (for wearing under sheer tops)
2 woollen singlets
4 pairs of socks
2 pairs of PJs
1 swimsuit
2 hats (1 summer, 1 winter)
2 sets of exercise gear (I do a load of washing
    every day so always have a clean set)

Tops

6 T-shirts/sleeveless tops
6 long-sleeved tops
1 woollen poncho (reversible)
3 blazers
1 denim jacket
1 leather jacket
1 warm jacket

Bottoms

2 pairs of jeans   2 skirts
    (1 black, 1 blue)   3 dresses
1 pair black pants   1 jumpsuit
2 pairs of shorts

Shoes

2 pairs of heels   1 pair of flats
1 pair of sandals   1 pair of sports shoes
1 pair of winter boots   1 pair of sneakers

Accessories

4 scarves
3 belts
3 necklaces
2 handbags

You could even take it to the next level by having a 'daily uniform'. Very smart over-achievers, such as Mark Zuckerberg and Steve Jobs, have claimed that wearing the same thing every day saves time and mental energy – and maybe, just maybe, it will help you build your own global empire (results may vary).

2. Second-hand

I feel like there's already enough clothing in the world, so I'm a big fan of buying second-hand. Twice a year (warm and cold seasons), I go to my favourite second-hand shop and buy a couple of new pieces for the season.

If there's something specific I need, I'll use the power of the Information Superhighway to find items. There are so many online platforms and social media groups now selling incredible second-hand gear.

Ask them to reuse something they already have to package it up.

3. Share

For special occasions and functions, I will often borrow and lend clothes with friends. I love the idea of my things getting used more! I'm also totally into renting clothes. There's a whole world out there when it comes to clothes rental, which means I can tap into all sorts of amazing clothes that I could never justify buying.

> @ **FIND IT ONLINE** Check out designerwardrobe.co.nz – you'll never need to rush to the mall before a special event again. Also check out great sites such as allthedresses.com, which acts as a search engine for various rental sites across Australia and NZ. So handy!

4. Buying new

For the few items that I do buy new (I draw the line at second-hand undies), all my other usual criteria start to kick in.

For example, when it comes to underwear, I will choose good-quality items that are made of GOTS certified organic cotton from a company that publishes details about their supply chain and ethics. I'll also consider how they make my bum look.

> ⊘ **TIME HACK** Get the app from goodonyou.eco
> to help you navigate clothing brands.

Repair/love/alter

As part of my fashion sustainability journey, I found myself in a new relationship. Her name is June. She is a magician masquerading as a tailor. I take her my clothes and she nips, tucks and magics them into something more fabulous. June's also brilliant at fixing and hemming things that are beyond my Year 8 sewing skills.

I have a girl crush on June.

Because I love the stuff I have and don't have a lot of it, I'm totally down with getting it repaired or altered. Even Prince Charles is a big fan of getting his suits repaired … hey, if it's good enough for the Royals!

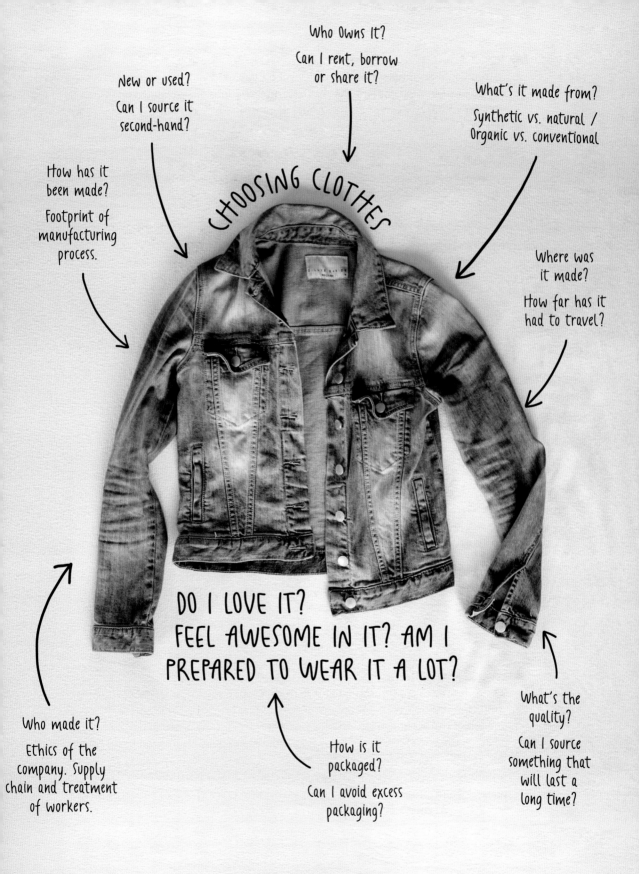

CHOOSING CLOTHES

Who Owns It?
Can I rent, borrow or share it?

New or used?
Can I source it second-hand?

What's it made from?
Synthetic vs. natural /
Organic vs. conventional

How has it been made?
Footprint of manufacturing process.

Where was it made?
How far has it had to travel?

DO I LOVE IT?
FEEL AWESOME IN IT? AM I
PREPARED TO WEAR IT A LOT?

Who made it?
Ethics of the company. Supply chain and treatment of workers.

How is it packaged?
Can I avoid excess packaging?

What's the quality?
Can I source something that will last a long time?

A good tailor is on par with a good hairdresser – if you find one, treat them like gold. I'm sure we've all had a bad jean-hemming experience that we don't need to go through again.

Washing your stuff

I have great news … we wash our clothes too much! Along with the energy and chemical impacts of over-washing, it also increases wear and tear, and releases microfibres from a number of synthetic fabrics.

→ For more information, see 'Clean' chapter, page 104.

> **A NOTE ON MICROFIBRES** In 2011, researchers Browne and colleagues found that washing one synthetic garment releases approx. 2,000 plastic microfibres. Because they're so small (less than 1 mm) microfibres often make their way through wastewater treatment plants and enter our rivers, lakes and even the ocean. Studies are now looking at how they're infiltrating our food chain. Search online for 'microfibre washing bag'.

> ⊘ **TIME HACK** Only wash your clothes when they really need it. Spot clean, air them out or spritz with vodka to keep things fresh between washing.

Whenever I buy something – either new or second-hand – I always wash it. I'm never quite sure what dyes and synthetic chemicals have been used in making the new items, or who has been wearing the second-hand ones – so we have a non-negotiable rule of 'washing before wearing' in our home! Even though it's not always easy to wait when I have kids (or me) excited about wearing new clothes.

Apart from that, I wash clothes when they need to be washed – not just because I've finished wearing them. Even the CEO of Levi Strauss & Co. says you don't need to wash your jeans ever; they wear better if you don't. You can bang them in the freezer, or I'm a fan of giving mine a regular airing on the clothesline and a spot cleaning.

There are special laundry bags out there, which you can use to reduce the amount of escapee plastic microfibres. Washing at colder temperatures will also release fewer fibres, as will washing with a full load (due to less friction).

What about the hit?

I was once asked how I fill the gaping void left by not feeling that rush of instant gratification from buying new clothes all the time. I still buy clothes – I'm just more intentional about how much, what it is and how I source it.

Here's how I still feel the hit. I was coming to the point of needing to replace my sneakers. Instead of rushing out to buy a new pair, I just waited. During my winter shop at my favourite second-hand store, I found a pair in my size that had never been worn! They were a quarter of the price of new ones. That hit of delayed gratification was epic.

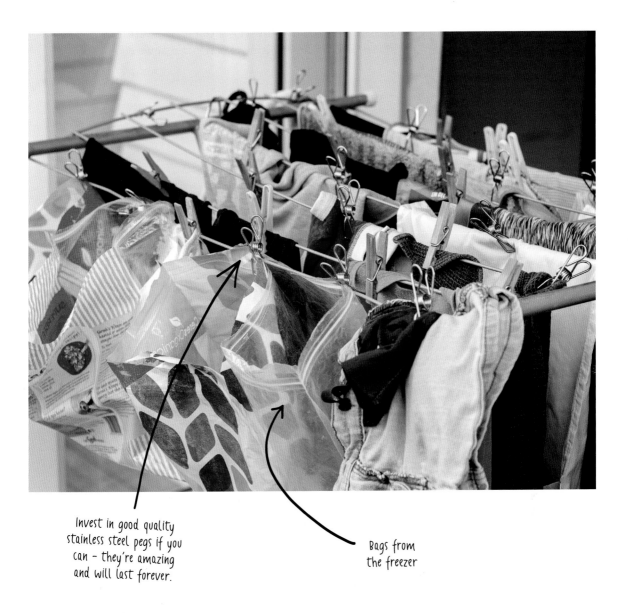

Invest in good quality stainless steel pegs if you can – they're amazing and will last forever.

Bags from the freezer

If you can take a pause before rushing out and buying something new, you'll make better choices, which will still scratch your gratification itch. And knowing that I'm making a better choice actually intensifies my sense of satisfaction.

I found that removing myself from the loop of temptation has also been a big win – you don't miss things when they're not in your face. It helps to escape the pressure of feeling that you're a season behind in the cut of your jeans, or that your skirt is the wrong length. I don't go window-shopping, I don't sign up for fashion marketing communications and, if I do ever spot something I want, I sleep on it to allow my rational brain to kick in.

CASE STUDY: LIZ'S SECOND-HAND STYLE TIPS

This is my friend Liz Viviani. Liz is a stylist who is passionate about second-hand fashion. I met her because she works at the preloved clothing shop where I'm a regular. She's my go-to for an honest opinion on what suits me, or what looks a bit mumsy.

Liz has given me some awesome tips for how to make the most of buying second-hand clothes:

- Know what fabrics and colours suit you. Most second-hand clothing shops are sorted by colour, so you can easily skip whole racks to save time.
- Don't let sizes deter you – because items have been worn, they may have changed shape, so it's worth trying them on. I've bought jeans a size below what I'd normally wear because of this.
- Sometimes, all you need to transform a look is a belt, a pop of colour from some statement jewellery or a killer heel.
- To find your personal style, know what you like and dress for your shape. Style has nothing to do with owning the latest 'must have' item and everything to do with being confident, individual and wearing what you love – and that's from a stylist!

Liz, the amazing second-hand stylist

How it goes out

I've got a pretty good swapping circle with a group of girlfriends. We get together for a weekend away once a year, and everyone brings anything they're done with. Organised clothes swaps are also starting to become a bit of a thing – so check out if there are any happening near you.

I sell clothes or put them on Pay It Forward pages, and I also donate to charity shops (only if it's something that is of a good-enough standard that other people would want to wear it).

For clothes that are past it, I cut them into cleaning cloths. Anything that is a natural fibre is cut up and added to the compost bin or worm farm.

One time, my neighbour caught me composting my husband's undies. It was awkward.

Slow your fashion

Fashion is a pretty personal, emotional and complex topic. If I was to find a one-size-fits-all approach for everyone, I would go with:

'Slow your fashion.'

Slowing my fashion and becoming more intentional has made me value my clothes so much more (cue teenage memories of my 501s). I like my wardrobe and feel good in what I wear. Sure, each purchase may take a bit more thought, but the fact that I'm buying so much less has saved me ridiculous amounts of time and money. I also love that kinda warm feeling I get from knowing that I'm reducing my impact by making better choices.

Even Anna Wintour does the same with her tendency for mid-length colourful dresses. Just saying!

THE SPOTLIGHT EFFECT Are you worried about people judging your small wardrobe? This is known as the 'spotlight effect' – our tendency to overestimate how much other people notice, or judge, our behaviour and appearance. If you think people are going to judge you for wearing the same generic black pants two days in a row – think again. Most people don't really notice, let alone care. They're too busy worrying about what other people think about their own pants.

BUSY TIPS – WHERE TO START?

- Next time you're heading to a special event, look at borrowing or renting something to wear.
- Get you mates over for a couple of wines and do a clothes swap.
- Before you buy something, ask yourself if you really love it.
- If you're buying something new, download the 'goodonyou' app to help make a better choice.

KIDS

'If you want your children to turn out well, spend twice as much time with them and half as much money.' – **ABIGAIL VAN BUREN**

When I was pregnant for the first time, there was a spreadsheet doing the rounds of a lot of my friends – it may still be circling in cyberspace to this day. This spreadsheet became my checklist, and I added a traffic light coding system for ease of project management (*I'm a traffic light and bullet point kinda gal*). Everything on that list needed to be a brilliant shade of green before my little human exited the womb.

I researched, price-compared, borrowed and bought. Target achieved, my daughter came into the world with everything she could possibly need, want or desire. I was winning at this parenting thing.

Six years in, and I've figured out that parenting actually has very little to do with that stuff. Beyond the basic necessities of life, and what is deemed to be socially acceptable, kids can get by with a surprisingly small amount of stuff. Simplifying what they have not only makes life easier and reduces your impact, but I've found that it has also fostered more creativity in my kids.

THE MINDSET

Raising eco-conscious kids

When I think about reducing my impact, raising eco-conscious kids is actually a massive part of what I can contribute. If I can do my bit to enable two more humans in the world to make a difference, then I'll be stoked.

My mission is to instil in my kids an understanding of how everything is connected, and an awareness of the impact that our actions have on other people and the world. I want my kids to appreciate the true value of things, people and experiences (along with all the other parental goals of having happy, healthy and content offspring).

Bring them with you

I've been told that I'm lucky I started this journey when my kids were young – and maybe I was. But I don't feel like I'd do it any differently if they were older.

I role model what I believe is right and bring them with me on the journey. I explain to them why I do things and why I make the choices I do, and I encourage them to ask questions. I don't hide alternatives from them (okay, sometimes, I intentionally walk the other way to avoid free balloons) but would rather they understand what choices there are and why we choose what we do. They don't always get it but I'm surprised at how often they do. I also find that kid-splaining things helps to keep things straight in my own head!

Several of my friends joke about my kids rebelling against me when they're older by becoming hoarders or starting an oil-fracking business. Watch this space.

Letting go

I'm figuring out that a large part of any parenting journey is learning to let go. As my kids get older and more independent, enabling them to have the right mindset makes me feel like they're more likely to go out into the world and make conscious decisions.

We talk about the decisions they make and I try, with all my motherly might, to never guilt-trip them about any choices they've made. I think that I pull it off, most of the time.

I don't unnecessarily try to shelter them or stop them experiencing the realities of consumerism – they have been inside a shopping mall. I think it's more important for them to be exposed to things and know how to navigate them. I also believe in the theory that what we do most of the time is what matters.

NAVIGATING BIRTHDAY PARTIES My six-year-old went to a birthday party where the kids were having Happy Meals. Now, I'm not going to say she can't have one, if that's what everyone else is getting. She loved the excitement of it! After she got home, we had a chat about the party. She told me that, next time, if she went to a party and they had Happy Meals, she'd ask to skip the plastic toy – but she really liked the chips. I was totally down with that.

OWNERSHIP AND ACCOUNTABILITY

A couple of years ago, when I was driving my then-four-year-old daughter to a birthday party, we had the following conversation:

> **ME:** I didn't realise Maggie's family are farmers.
> **FOUR-YEAR-OLD:** Just like us.
> **ME:** What do you mean?
> **FOUR-YEAR-OLD:** We're worm farmers.

The kids love when they have a bit of ownership. Every time there's been a pet day at pre-school, my kids rock up with their jar of worms and proudly show them off.

GETTING IT DONE

Toys

When it comes to toys, more is not more. There are only so many toys kids can play with. Research by toy supplier Dream Town found that the average 10-year-old owns 238 toys but plays with just 12 of them daily. It's disturbing how many of them end up at the bottom of the toy box, unloved and forgotten. There's also been a heap of studies that show how having fewer toys can inspire innovation and creativity.

I see this creativity in my own kids. One day, a simple plank of wood kept my two kids amused for hours. It was a shop counter, flight control desk, keyboard and ramp for cars. I'm not saying we should replace all toys with planks of wood and a handful of rocks; I've just learned that it's important to let play happen, instead of facilitating it with every toy for every whim.

'As you decrease the quantity of your child's toys and clutter, you increase their attention and their capacity for deep play.' – **KIM JOHN PAYNE**

Two kids, one box

We have one toy box for all of the kids' toys (excluding bikes and a few other things). If it doesn't fit in the toy box, something needs to be passed on. I will mostly go for quality toys that foster imagination or get them active, and will often try to source them second hand.

> ⊘ **TIME HACK** Fewer toys means so much less tidying up, sorting and organising, and my frustration levels are so much less!

Sharing toys

Every other week, we visit the toy library and rent a few items to give the kids some variety (on alternating weeks, we'll go to the book library).

The library toys get so much love from so many kids; it's such a cool way to cut down the amount of stuff they have. The kids love running into mates at the library and chatting about the different toys. They get such a buzz, knowing they're all playing with the same things.

> @ **FIND IT ONLINE** There are hundreds of toy libraries across NZ and Australia. Check out toylibrary.co.nz and toylibraries.org.au.

> ⊘ **TIME HACK** Always having a fresh stash of toys or books from the library entertains my kids for hours on the weekend.

If you have older kids, consider a sharing or swapping circle with friends and family.

Rental system

If the kids are with me at the charity shop, I'll often let them choose one toy each to buy. We're now in the habit of making up stories about who owned the toy before they did, which they love doing! When we get home, they choose one of their toys to pass on and we put it aside for next time we go to the charity shop. Things just keep going around and around – I love the fact that it's like a rental system and that it also supports a local charity.

Clothes

Have what they need

When I was growing up, I'm pretty sure I had three pairs of corduroy pants, two jumpers, four T-shirts and a party dress. I definitely had only one pair of shoes per season, plus some gumboots. It's not that I went without, clothes just weren't as easy to come by, and so, we only had what we needed.

My kids have a few more clothes than that, but not by a lot. They don't really need that much – they always end up wearing the same favourites anyway. I'm also amazed at my daughter's creativity at pulling together different ensembles using the same few favourite items. My son is happy alternating between his three superhero T-shirts and wearing any pair of shorts (regardless of the season).

KIDS CLOTHING ITEMS

One set of clothes is only to be worn for special occasions.
List excludes specific items like dance uniforms and sports gear.

General

6 pairs of underwear
4 merino/cotton singlets
6 pairs of socks (my kids lost
so many gloves, they now just
wear socks on their hands)
2 pairs of PJs
1 swimsuit
2 hats (1 summer, 1 winter)

Tops

4 T-shirts
4 long-sleeved tops
3 hoodies or sweatshirts
1 casual jacket
1 warm jacket

Bottoms

3 pairs of long pants
(completely pointless for my son)
3 pairs of shorts

Shoes

1 pair of gumboots
1 pair of sneakers
1 pair of boots/sandals

Additional items,
if your child wants

2 skirts
3 dresses

⊘ **TIME HACK** Reducing the amount of clothes my kids have makes it easy for them to find specific items, keeps their drawers tidier, and has the added benefit of keeping the washing pile manageable!

Sourcing clothes

I buy mainly second-hand clothes or I'm given hand-me-downs from friends and family. When I do buy new, I'll choose good-quality items that will last. For items such as gumboots and basics, I'll choose unisex options that will last for both my kids, and can be easily passed on when we're done with them.

> ⊙ **TIME HACK** I go to the second-hand shop (or online) twice a year
> to find what the kids need for the season. Having both a boy and girl,
> choosing good-quality unisex items means I only need to buy them once.

Passing them on

Because my kids don't have a lot of clothing items, they're normally pretty spent at the end of each season. Anything that is still in good condition continues on the carousel of hand-me-downs or is donated. For any items that are past the point of no return, I cut them up for cleaning cloths; natural fibres can then be composted (just make sure they don't have any added synthetic materials, buttons, zippers, etc.).

Baby stuff

Nappies

If you're still at the nappy stage with your kids, moving to a reusable cloth option will save you a huge amount of money and waste. (It's estimated that, on average, a child will go through about 5,000 disposable nappies in their lifetime, costing roughly $4,000. A new set of cloth nappies will set you back about $1,000.) Even with a bit of extra cost for washing, you'd still be way better off.

Panic not: no longer do you need to origami a pink-edged cotton square into an enormous wad and fasten it with a menacing looking 'safety' pin.

Modern cloth nappies fit like disposables and are made of high-performance fabrics – they also look pretty darn cute with lots of different colours and patterns. The biggest challenge is actually navigating all of the different choices, because there are just so many.

I used cloth for both of my kids most of the time – although I didn't start until my daughter was one. It doesn't matter when you start. The hardest thing was beginning (it's so easy to overthink things and read too much on the interweb), but then it became part of life's daily rhythm.

Thankfully, the preschool my kids attend is very supportive of cloth nappies. I just drop off enough clean nappies for each day, along with a waterproof bag for storing the used nappies, then collect the bag at the end of the day.

Remember: it doesn't have to be an all-or-nothing game. Even replacing a disposable with a cloth nappy once a day will save 365 disposable nappies from going to landfill every year!

Added benefit: in summertime, cloth nappies totally look like shorts.

NIC'S CLOTH NAPPY ROUTINE

Of course, follow any manufacturers' instructions.

- Remove any solids from the nappy (or 'not so solids' when it came to my kids).

- Store nappies in a lidded bucket (no need to soak these days).

- Every second day, do a pre-wash and then a normal wash cycle with regular detergent at 40–60°C.

- Line dry – the sunlight will help to 'bleach' out stains.

- I also used muslin/cheesecloth squares for reusable wipes. To use, I just ran them under a tap first, then washed with the nappies.

⊙ TIME HACKS FOR GETTING STARTED

- Start by trialling just one nappy. It's tempting to want to go out and buy a whole stash … but reusables are only good if you actually reuse them. I know a heap of people who have pristine sets of never-used cloth nappies sitting in cupboards!

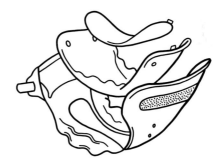

- Find a local nappy retailer and ask if they do a trial set of nappies, or just ask what their most popular style is and start with one of those.

- Ask around – you'll probably find at least one of your friends, or someone in your baby coffee group, has one they're willing to lend you.

- Find a Pay It Forward cloth nappy group, like the amazing one at Raising Ziggy: raisingziggy.com/cloth-nappies-free.

- Look online for second-hand sets of cloth nappies – you'll need about 25 nappies if you're using them full time. There's even Facebook groups dedicated to 'modern cloth nappies' where you can also buy and sell.

- Get to a workshop. Local councils will often fund education initiatives, so get in touch and see if there's anything happening in your area.

@ **FIND IT ONLINE** Check out more resources at: katemeads.co.nz, raisingziggy.com and australiannappyassociation.org.au.

Baby food

I applied my batch-cooking philosophy to baby food as well. I'd batch-cook lots of dishes, then freeze small portions in ice-cube trays (and later, in muffin trays).

My best investment was a 'fresh food feeder' – this is a mesh bag that you can put fresh food in. The baby then sucks at the food through the mesh. The food didn't need any prepping and the feeder was so handy to have when we were out and about to save me from buying packets.

Reusables for me

Reusable breast pads and period undies saved me so much money after I had my babies. Having these items was also great time saver – once I'd bought them I was sorted.

School

When my daughter started school, life went up a notch. She's now surrounded by lots of friends, who roll a bit differently to us. She's exposed to a lot more temptation and comparison – there are more parties, more stuff, more events. I don't want her to feel like she doesn't fit in, but I also don't want to revert how we do things, if there can be a better way.

The way we navigate school life is no different from what we do at home – we have lots of conversations and figure out alternatives and compromises together. We make better choices where we can.

When my daughter starts comparing what she has to others, for instance, it's a chance to have a conversation about the choices we make as a family. Sometimes, it motivates us to plan something fun to do together, so she can connect with the value of experiences.

Of course, nutrition is a bigger priority, and we only made the change because it works for us to supply the milk ourselves.

BETTER SCHOOL MILK My daughter's school is part of the 'milk for schools' program. Every afternoon, she was loving the novelty of having her tetrapack of milk. She'd often bring these cartons home and we'd make sure to take the empties back to the dedicated bins at school, as there's a great recycling program for them.

Then one day, she said she really liked getting the milk, but it made quite a bit of rubbish. We had a chat and decided she'd like to take her own milk to school in a reusable thermos. She got to choose her own thermos, she's really into it, and we both feel way better about the waste.

⊘ **TIME HACK** Get your kids involved. The deal with my daughter taking her own milk to school is that she has to fill the thermos herself every morning.

Stainless steel drink bottles and lunchboxes last really well

So many cool cloth nappy designs

Homemade playdough

Handmade book bag (not made by me, though)

Toy library goodness

Unlacquered coloured pencils = compost friendly

Food storage

- Lunchboxes: I invested in stainless steel lunchboxes five years ago and they're still going strong. I went for compartment-style ones and both the kids also have lunch bags, so we can add other containers and ice packs when needed.
→ For lunchbox food inspo, see page 62.
- Beeswax wraps: I'll use these for wraps, sandwiches and cut fruit. When they start looking a bit manky, I just put them on an oven tray in a 100°C oven for 2 minutes.
- Drink bottles: We roll with stainless steel drink bottles because they don't taint the water, unlike plastic can. They get a bit dinged up, but they last for years.

> ⊙ **TIME HACK** Kids' reusables such as lunchboxes and drink bottles make great gift ideas for Christmas and birthdays.

Supplies

Stationery

The first time I received a stationery list from school, we diligently went out and bought everything on it. Now, we don't. We chat to the teachers about alternatives, bring home items from the previous year and reuse them, find items at home, and then fill in the gaps by buying where we need to. When we do buy stationery, we look for alternatives such as refillable pens, items made with recycled materials, unlacquered pencils, metal scissors, wooden rulers and handmade bookbags (made by other people, not me).

It's also worth checking out the local op shop.

> ⊙ **TIME HACK** Chat to the school and see if they're keen to gather unused resources at the end of the school year and make these available to save everyone buying it all over again.

School bags

Both my kids were given school bags for Christmas one year. I looked at locally made ones, and options that were made from natural or recycled fabrics, but I ended up choosing a really good-quality option that comes with a lifetime guarantee. My plan is to never have to buy a school bag again, and a couple of years in, we're tracking well!

Events

Sausage sizzles and school discos are regular fundraisers at our school. My daughter knows that she can choose one thing and her options are the low-waste goodies, such as a sausage in bread instead of a plastic-wrapped cookie.

There are lots of great low-waste alternatives for school fundraisers out there. I've heard of discos where they ditch the glowsticks for glow-in-the-dark face paint, and switch packaged snacks for a popcorn machine and a soda stream station. If you're up for it, suggest alternative ideas. Just know that timing is everything and even if things don't change straight away, you've planted the seed.

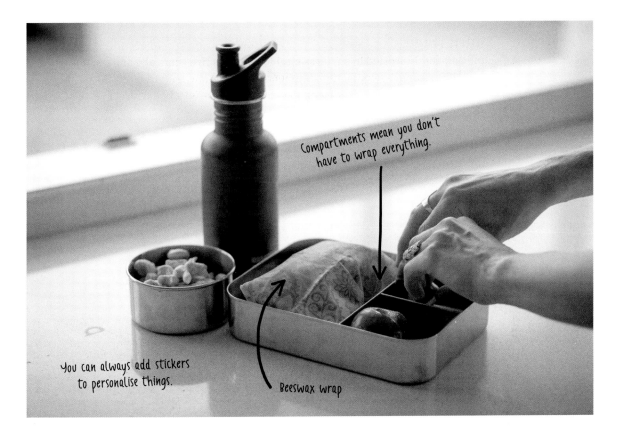

Compartments mean you don't have to wrap everything.

You can always add stickers to personalise things.

Beeswax wrap

Keep it simple

As a parent, there's an inbuilt desire to provide everything you can for your child. In the developed world, there's no shortage of options – every whim is available at the click of the mouse or the tap of a credit card. Sometimes, I feel a bit like I'm going against the grain when I limit what my kids have – but when I let go of what other people think and reconnect with my 'why', I know I'm on track, and man, does it make life simpler.

Check out the following chapter, 'Gifts + Celebrations', for gift and party ideas.

BUSY TIPS – WHERE TO START?

- Visit your local toy library and do a trial borrow.
- Sit down with your kids and explain the changes you're making and get them on board.
- Get your kids to choose one toy or item of clothing to pass along to someone (encourage them to write a note to the new owner).

GIFTS +
CELEBRATIONS

'Life is what you celebrate.' – JOANNE HARRIS

Giving gifts and having celebrations are such an awesome part of being human – they bring people together, create connection and show affection. They are what life is all about.

I want my family's life to be always full of celebration and giving – who doesn't? What I've figured out, however, is that this doesn't have to be about elaborate parties and enormous piles of gifts – that just stresses everyone out, costs heaps and ain't great for the planet. Being mindful of your impact and the choices you're making opens up a whole world of wondrous and simple alternatives.

GIFTS AND GIVING

THE MINDSET

In 1992, a guy called Gary wrote an insightful (and very purple-coloured) book called *The Five Love Languages*. This book was about the different ways people experience and express love. Some of us are into physical touch, whereas others prefer quality time or words of affirmation.

In case you're interested – mine is 'acts of service' (do the vacuuming or make me dinner, and you're in).

I find a brilliant irony in the fact that my mother's love language is 'gift giving'. Yep, giving ... stuff.

Given that living with less is my thing, the easiest way to control gift-giving would be to put a blanket ban on anybody buying stuff for our family. Would it get me the outcome of less stuff? Yep. Would I upset and p!ss other people off? For sure. Would I be better off? No.

For me, nailing an approach to gift-giving is about recognising that there are two sides to every gift – giving and receiving. We need to accept that we're all different and we need to find ways to navigate this in a way that works for everyone.

The cool thing is that, if you really strip it back, giving is about human connection – it's about showing gratitude and love. (Not about plastic snowglobes and novelty reindeer jumpers!) Too often, we get caught up in the hype and pressure of consumption.

Reconnecting with the true intention of gift-giving has helped me to ground myself when I'm finding ways to make it work.

GETTING IT DONE

Less is more

It's kind of ironic that gifts are about gratitude and love, yet so many of us feel totally overwhelmed by it all. We're getting overwhelmed spending time, energy and money buying things for people and then, sometimes, they don't even want them!

> Most of us get up to three unwanted gifts at Christmastime.
> – Trade Me NZ survey

With this in mind, the first step in my gift-giving journey was to have conversations with people in my giving universe. Yep, good old-fashioned talking to people. It wasn't official, just as the opportunity arose; I would have a chat about whether people were keen to simplify things. I wasn't being a tight-arse or pushing people into it – it was just an open dialogue about the best way to approach things, a 'Hey, what do you think we do about presents this year?' Wouldn't you know it, everyone was keen to make life simpler – the relief on some people's faces was immense. I'm unclear if the motivation was to be given less stuff or to spend less time buying gifts, but hey, whatever works.

It's been an evolution, as people adjust to changes and then feel comfortable doing more (or in this case, less).

- For Christmas, we went from everyone buying something for everyone, to a Secret Santa approach, to now just buying one gift for each child (with only one awkward slip-up when someone didn't get the memo). As cheesy as it sounds, the focus is now more about just having time together.
- For birthdays, I have an agreement with my friends that, instead of birthday gifts, we'll just manage to actually hang out or catch up on a video call!

When it comes to our kids, we also keep things pretty simple. I love the concept of:

Something they want, something they need,
something to wear and something to read.

It's so easy to get carried away. I still feel the pang, a few days before Christmas or a birthday – that desire to do a midnight run to Kmart to get a few last-minute stocking fillers or extra bits. The feeling of dread: 'I don't have enough.' I've learned to tune out from that feeling – I always have enough.

⊘ **TIME HACK** Establishing a less-is-more approach to gift giving saves time, money and energy and allows you to focus more on people rather than things.

Simplifying gifts has made a huge difference to what I do, but I still give gifts (and like to be given them). Here are some of the ways I do things.

Experiences

This is always my first stop. What's better than creating memories with someone? From blacksmith courses to movie vouchers, kids' fluffy dates to skydiving – the possibilities are endless. You can also get a double bonus when you buy an experience for someone else and then get to be part of it, too!

Over the past few years, the 'go to' Christmas presents for my husband and me have been tickets to a summer festival. (The ones where it's not too weird if you're middle-aged and in bed by midnight.) Festivals are a great way to spend time together and it justifies dropping cash on something purely hedonistic. Sure, the element of surprise might be lacking, but we make sure we bring that in for birthdays.

For the kids, we take them to the circus, a one-on-one night away or horseback riding (or in our case, pony strolling). If we can't do the activity on the day, we create a bit of theatre and excitement around it by having clues that they need to guess.

I can sometimes get carried away with ideas, especially for big birthdays, but it can be as simple as a voucher for a coffee date (just make sure you follow through, otherwise you'll look a bit stink).

Traditions

Gifts

I'm always up for some ritual and tradition; it can be a nice way to find the middle ground for gift-giving. Each year, my mum will take my daughter shopping for a new pair of shoes for her birthday. They make an event of it and will normally go out for morning tea. I'm happy because my daughter gets something she needs; Mum's happy because she's given a gift; and my daughter is stoked because she gets to choose a new pair of shoes. It's also created a nice tradition they both really look forward to.

Mum has also taken to buying all the grandchildren winter PJs at Easter-time. I'm stoked because it skips all the sugar and packaging; the cousins love it because they all have matching PJs; and Mum gets her gift-itch scratched!

⊘ **TIME HACK** Creating gift traditions around things the kids need saves shopping time for everyone.

Food traditions

We've fallen into the rhythm of everyone in our immediate family having a 'special food' on their birthday. As a family, we spend time making and eating them together. (As I write this, I realise that we sound like the Brady Bunch – but if you ever saw the kitchen afterwards, you'd realise it's not nearly that romantic.)

For birthdays, my husband and son both receive an enormous custard square (→ see recipe, opposite), which must be eaten in bed at breakfast time; I get homemade sushi; and my daughter always chooses to go out for dinner somewhere.

On our wedding anniversary, we make homemade ice cream – it used to be a vaguely romantic affair where we'd come up with creative flavours (often involving alcohol) and eat it on the couch while watching a movie. Now, the kids are involved.

Time and skills

In a world where time is one of the most precious commodities we have, giving it is a pretty freaken awesome thing to do. Using your time to share a skill is also a sure-fire way to make you (or the skill-giver) feel pretty damn good. I've heard of grandparents who have painted or wallpapered kids' rooms and I've helped friends minimise their wardrobes. My father-in-law has made the kids a mud-kitchen, zhuzhed-up second-hand bikes and made our raised garden beds.

Recipe: Custard squares

YOU WILL NEED

1 packet vanilla instant dessert (I grew up calling this 'instant pudding')

1 litre cream (ideally, in a returnable glass bottle)

two 30 cm x 30 cm squares of pastry (→ for my Very very rough pastry
 recipe, see page 59)

25 g butter, melted

½ cup icing sugar

2 tablespoons passionfruit pulp (optional) (when they're in season,
 I freeze passionfruit pulp in ice-cube trays)

WHAT TO DO

1. In a bowl, add instant dessert powder and cream. Whip mixture until
thick then put in the fridge for 30 minutes. While that's chilling, preheat
the oven to 180°C.

2. Place the two sheets of pastry onto baking trays and cook in the oven
for about 15 minutes.

3. Remove pastry from the oven and, with a clean tea towel, carefully
press to make them flat.

4. To make the icing, in a small bowl, mix melted butter and icing
sugar together, adding water or extra icing sugar to reach the correct
consistency.

5. Once pastry is cool, top one sheet with icing. Cut this sheet into
16 squares (it makes cutting the cake so much easier when it's finished).
Load bottom sheet of pastry with the cream mixture.

6. Assemble the cut pastry pieces over the top, and respread the icing
to cover the cut marks. Drizzle the custard squares with passionfruit.
Keep in the fridge and eat for breakfast.

Preloved gifts

Buying preloved

I'm a big fan of sourcing second-hand gifts for my kids. They love the concept that their stuff has had a history with another child, and love passing things on for the same reason. For items such as bikes, buying used also gives you an insight into its quality. Buying something new often means you don't know how it will wear.

Passing it on

At Christmas, older cousins have sometimes chosen a toy they've outgrown to pass down – the kids love it! Keeping it in the family also helps overcome the mental barrier of buying second hand for some people.

Among our friends, the philosophy of hand-me-downs is a large part of the way we give gifts. Our good clothes, bikes and toys are passed on and shared. (A friend even held onto a toy truck that I'd given to her son and gave it to my son 15 years later).

> **TOP PACKAGING TIP** When I buy second-hand items (or anything) online, I'll always ask if people have packaging lying around that they can reuse, instead of using a new plastic courier bag.

Handmade and upcycling

This is normally the section I'd skip over, because it feels like it doesn't really fit with my ideal of simplifying or saving time. But I've figured out a way to crack handmade gifts, without it feeling like a mission.

Since having kids, I've discovered that there is a birthday-party season every year. Now, at the beginning of each birthday season, my kids and I get prepared by making a big batch of birthday presents for their friends. Some favourites have been terrariums, bath bombs and recipes in a jar. The activity takes us a couple of hours, is fun to do together and the kids love giving something they have made.

> ⊘ **TIME HACK** Bulk gift-making has saved a heap of time, stress and money, versus all those last-minute panicked trips to the shops I was previously making. I always ended up spending more than I wanted, buying cheap crap and putting it in a glossy (non-compostable) gift bag.

I'm also getting into the habit of making gifts in bulk for Christmas. I normally make something in a glass jar or bottle, because I always have a massive stash. I've made vanilla essence (→ for recipe, see page 64), and Limoncello and Chai latte mix (see recipes, opposite). If they don't get used for gifts, my back-up plan is to consume them myself!

Recipe: Chai latte mix

WHAT YOU'LL NEED FOR 1 JAR

8 teaspoons ground ginger
6 teaspoons ground cinnamon
3 teaspoons ground nutmeg
3 teaspoons ground allspice
1 teaspoon ground cloves
½ teaspoon ground cardamom
8 teaspoons coconut sugar
(optional, to desired sweetness)

WHAT TO DO
Put in a clean jar, shake well.
How to use: Place 1 teaspoon in a mug.
Add hot milk of choice.

Recipe: Limoncello

WHAT YOU'LL NEED FOR SIX 250 ML BOTTLES

the peel and juice of 10 unwaxed lemons (without the pith)
1 litre bottle of vodka
1½ cups water
1 cup sugar

WHAT TO DO
1. Place lemon peel in a large clean jar. Pour over vodka and cover with a tight-fitting lid. Leave mixture to steep in a dark place for about 2 weeks – ideally giving it a gentle shake every day (or when you remember).
2. In a small saucepan over medium heat, boil water, sugar and lemon juice until mixture is syrupy. Allow to cool to room temperature.
3. Strain the lemon peel from the vodka, then mix the vodka into the syrup. Decant limoncello into small clean bottles.
How to use: Serve chilled or over ice.

Buying new

Local makers

When I do buy new items, I try to source local products directly from the maker, or support local businesses.

> **@ FIND IT ONLINE** If you don't want to leave your couch, check out websites such as etsy.com (filter by geography), madeit.com.au or felt.co.nz.

GIFTS BRINGING PEOPLE TOGETHER

Or, gifts that foster doing fun stuff are a great idea. One year, I sourced a whole lot of games from my childhood second-hand. It's so cool, being able to play Guess Who, Connect 4 and Battleship with my kids. I've got friends who are building their camping empire more and more each year. They love going on camping trips as a family and, every birthday and Christmas, give each other another thing they need!

Last Christmas, I gave my daughter a *Wreck this Journal* and we spent a couple of weeks over the summer holidays doing activities from it together.

Sorry – this is all pretty gross, but man did we laugh.

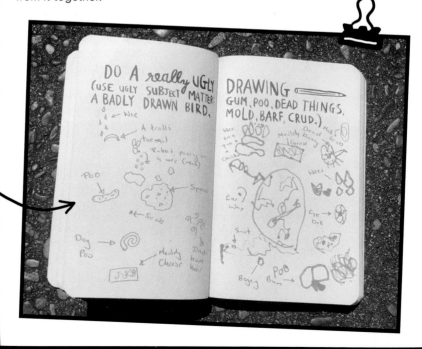

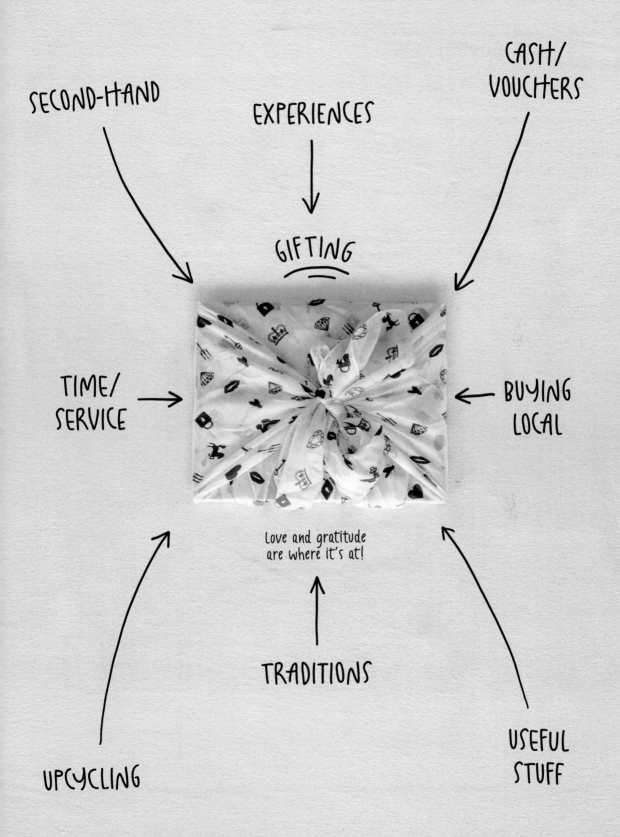

SECOND-HAND

EXPERIENCES

CASH/ VOUCHERS

GIFTING

TIME/ SERVICE

BUYING LOCAL

Love and gratitude are where it's at!

UPCYCLING

TRADITIONS

USEFUL STUFF

Fairy Garden – everything sourced from op shops and the garden

Salt dough decorations, see page 218 for recipe

Seed bombs, see page 220 for recipe

Furoshiki with op shop scarf

Nature makes the best decor.

Popcorn – thread on cotton for a decoration, or makes for a great zero-waste party snack.

Kids' artwork

Useful things

Good quality

I'm a fan of receiving and giving useful items that are great quality, which I could never justify buying just for myself. I've been bought an umbrella, a beautiful stovetop kettle, a refillable fountain pen and socks with a lifetime guarantee.

Keep a list

I always keep a list of stuff on my phone that my kids (or I) need or really want. Then, if anyone ever needs any gift ideas, I've got them at the ready. Writing down wishes on a list is also a good way to avoid the temptation of instant gratification.

Giving back

Lots of charities have ways to 'gift' a donation to someone else. Check out websites like thegoodregistry.com, where you can select from numerous charities. Such a great idea for corporate gifting, too.

Wrapping paper

Wrapping paper may not seem like a big deal, but it's designed to be single use, and often isn't recyclable (think mixed materials and plastic sticky tape). We're also consuming a heap of it. CARE Asturalia found that, in Australia alone, the wrapping paper used each Christmas could wrap around the Equator nearly four times.

I've got amongst the Japanese art of furoshiki. This is kind of like gift-wrapping origami with scarves or pieces of fabric. There's a way to fold for gifts of every shape. For family gifts, we have scarves in the kids' toybox that we use, or I'll grab a stash from the op shop to use on gifts for other people. Or you can use old sheets or any other fabric you have.

I save larger pieces of artwork that the kids make, or use old posters or magazines, to wrap items to post or give as gifts.

If I want things to look a bit fancy, I'll grab some foliage out of the garden – flowers, twigs or leaves are a great way to raise the bar on your wrapping skills.

Let it go

I don't always get it right when it comes to gifts. I have conversations where and when I feel is appropriate, and I role model what I believe in. But I've learned that I can't control everything and I need to let go of perfection. When all the planets align, it feels wicked, but when my kids or I are given something that is destined for landfill or the bottom of the toybox, I accept it and I'm grateful – I know it's come from a place of love and gratitude. Namaste.

CASE STUDY: COOL CHRISTMAS TRADITIONS

I love what my friend Nicole does for Christmas. Her two kids make potato-print paper for gift-wrapping and she also makes her own Christmas crackers! Such a cool family tradition – and reusing the toys from the crackers each year means no more crappy plastic whistles to annoy the hell out of everyone.

Nicole's gorgeous daughter Ayla

CELEBRATIONS

THE MINDSET

Whether it's a birthday, Christmas, or just a good old-fashioned knees-up, when I'm throwing a celebration, I keep the same conscious mindset that I do in my daily life. It's not about taking more time or making things more complex, I just make simple switches to reduce my impact.

Food

When you're in celebration mode, it's super easy for food packaging and food waste to get out of control. We're wanting to treat ourselves, and nobody wants to be the host of a party where the food is crap or it runs out!

Packaging

Making your own food is an obvious way to avoid packaging waste.

> ⊘ **TIME HACK** To save me time and effort, I keep things simple and don't go overboard with a heap of variety. I make a few dishes, but make them well, and make a lot of them.

For food items that I do buy, I'll try to find better alternatives from a packaging and ingredients perspective. Some of my go-tos are:

- Frozen sausage rolls in a compostable cardboard box
- Lollies, nuts and pretzels from the bulk bin section at the supermarket or a bulk food shop
- Homemade soda water drinks station (or I've been to fancy cocktail parties where they've had old-fashioned soda siphons)
- DIY popcorn for kids' parties – this has the added bonus that it makes the house smell like a movie theatre. Hiring popcorn machines is also a cool idea for a big event, or for something like a school disco.
- If I'm making a platter, I'll gather my bags and containers, and head to the market for produce, fruit, meats, cheeses and homemade relishes.

> ⊘ **TIME HACK** I'll often ask people to bring a plate in place of a gift. This both addresses the gift thing and helps take the pressure off me having to do all of the cooking myself. Double win.

When I book catering, I'll have a conversation with the supplier about avoiding any unnecessary waste. I've also dropped off my own containers in advance to avoid cling wrap or disposable trays and containers. (I just write my name and number on the containers to make their lives easier.)

Food waste

- I try not to over-cater. To avoid the risk of running out, I'll always have some back-ups on hand to pull out if I need them. I've been to plenty of parties where the back-up plan is to do a late-night pizza order when the food runs out – it goes down an absolute treat!
- I will always have a plan for leftovers. They are sent home with guests or used up for family meals, or I leave containers out so leftovers can easily be thrown in the freezer.
- Make sure you have bins out for people's food scraps so the scraps are easy to compost.

> ⊘ **TIME HACK** Have easy access to bins for recyclables and compost to save it going in the rubbish bin, and to save you having to pick through rubbish after the party.

Decorations

At our house, we have generic celebration bunting. I bought it online and it's been upcycled from old blankets. The bunting is hung across the lounge for any relevant festivity. I love the fact it's created a simple tradition that the kids love and that marks the observance of something important.

> ⊘ **TIME HACK** Going for reusable decorations means you only have to buy the bunting once.

A friend of mine has had bunting made for each of her kids from their old baby clothes and blankets.

Nature is also a pretty awesome source of decorations. Flowers, leaves, pinecones, wreathes or even confetti made out of dried leaves are all favourites at our place. To clean up, just throw it all back into the garden!

I also go natural when it comes to candles, choosing a natural beeswax option – they smell so good.

Our Christmas tree is an outdoor potted plant, which comes in and is decorated each year. If you've got an artificial one, keep on using it as long as you can. Each year, we go to the local Christmas craft festival; the kids choose one decoration each and we write the year on it. Then we use ribbons and scarves that we already have at home, and the kids bake and decorate salt dough shapes (→ recipe page 218).

My husband is a planner and really wanted a whiteboard. Given my minimalist tendencies, I suggested that, instead, he could get a liquid chalk pen and write on the windows. The upside is that we can now decorate the windows with pictures and messages for parties and Christmas. The kids love doing it, and I love the simplicity of wiping it off when we're done!

Reusables

There's a fascinating human behaviour I've observed when it comes to reusables such as crockery, cutlery and serviettes … people will use less of it compared to disposables. I don't know if it's a respect thing, or an acknowledgement of the fact they need to be washed – whatever it is, it's pretty cool. I also swear that things taste better on a real plate and eaten with proper cutlery.

Crockery and cutlery

For large parties, it's easy to hire crockery, glasses and cutlery. I tend to treat my local charity shop like a rental service – I'll stock up on what I need, then return it a few days later. They'll always do me a deal if I'm buying a lot and it's getting too expensive; returning the stock later means they get to sell it all over again. The added bonus is that you don't have a set deadline that you need to return it by!

For kids' parties, check out your local toy library. They sometimes have sets you can hire.

> ⊘ **TIME HACK** Some groups of friends have a 'party set' of plates, which gets passed around to be used at every different celebration.

Napkins

You'll be amazed at how few are used if you go with a reusable cloth option! For kids' parties, I just have a stash of my general cloths on hand (the ones made out of cut-up clothes).

Straws

If you can get away with skipping straws altogether, that's the easiest option. Otherwise, opt for reusables if it's practical, or source paper ones and throw them in the compost.

When someone wants to bring a gift

When you're hosting a celebration, gift-giving can take a different form. To honour people's desire to give a gift (or feel justified in not giving one) here are some of the things that I've done that have gone down pretty well:

- Go with the 'bring a plate of food' in place of a gift (and save on cooking)
- For our wedding, we asked people to give us a bottle of wine, which we would cellar, then drink together later. This gave us a reason to get together with all of our guests and enjoy fun times again.
- If I'm asking people to not bring presents, I try to give them a reason. Here's the wording from my joint birthday celebration with a friend:

> Gifts: Don't even think about it – for real. Liz has too much sh!t and Nic is a converted minimalist.

Get the kids involved – it's messy but fun!

Recipe: Salt dough decorations

YOU WILL NEED

4 cups four
1 cup salt
1½ cups water

WHAT TO DO

1. Preheat the oven to 160°C.
2. Mix all ingredients together in a bowl. Place on a clean work surface and knead until smooth.
3. Roll out dough, cut into shapes and create a small hole for hanging. Place shapes on baking trays, then cook in the oven for about 25 minutes.
4. Remove shapes from the oven and allow to cool. Decorate (go for compost-friendly choices such as natural paints and bio-glitter), adding cotton thread or natural twine for hanging.
5. When you've finished enjoying them, simply compost.

Kids' parties

Gifts

As a parent, I know my life is a whole lot easier if I have some guidance on what to give a child for their birthday. Read your audience and decide if it's the right approach for you, but here are a few ideas:

- Have a themed party such as a garden party, where guests are asked to bring a plant, or a baking party, where they're asked to bring a recipe.
- Throw a 'fiver' party, where guests bring $5 in place of a gift, and the money goes towards one larger present or an experience.
- One child desperately wanted to go to a theme park so, for his birthday, his parents set up a themed money-box and people had the option of contributing towards the experience in place of a gift.
- If you're asked for ideas, use that list on your phone for items your kids really need or want.
- A friend's teenage son blew her away when he asked his friends to bring gifts of their old toys and books, which he then donated to a local children's charity.

I get that money is polarising, so you should always give people options.

> **BURSTING BALLOONS** Some balloons claim to be biodegradable – but details are sketchy about how long they take to break down. Without sounding like the fun police, the best thing we can do is avoid them. I skip balloons at our parties and, if at all humanly possible, I try to turn them down when we're out and about and the kids are offered them – especially the ones on plastic sticks! I succumbed once to avoid what was on track to be an epic two-year-old meltdown – you need to pick your battles.

Invitations

When it comes to invitations, I'm all for going digital but, sometimes, there's nothing like receiving an envelope in the post or having something to put on the fridge. If I am choosing a physical invite, I usually upcycle something or make sure I pick materials that are easily recyclable or compostable – I skip invitations that have lots of plastic pearls, pop-up butterflies, ribbons or other forms of bejazzling on it.

Goodie bags

When I was growing up and going to parties, I remember it was the norm to be sent home with a piece of the birthday cake in a paper serviette – two pieces if you were lucky and they knew you had a sibling (*although, I think I always ate my brother's piece as well*). Goodie bags have become a bit of a thing, both at kids' parties and weddings. You can, of course, skip them but, if you're into them, here are some ideas that will avoid setting foot in a dollar store.

> ⊙ **TIME HACK** Think goodies that mean you don't need to make a special shopping trip.

- Go with something edible – stick with the birthday cake plan, or reuse some old jars, allowing your guests to fill them up with treats to take away.
- Homemade thank-you cards are a lovely way to show a sense of gratitude towards your guests.
- At one party, we gave away seed bombs, which were a huge hit. You can either buy them or make them yourself. Seed bombs can be thrown anywhere where there's a bit of soil and they will sprout into a burst of wildflowers.
- Another simple change is to give gifts that can be reused, upcycled or are just low waste. We've made beeswax wraps as gifts, and given coloured pencil sets and squares of old magazine paper with origami instructions.

There's even a thing called 'Guerrilla Gardening', where people throw seed bombs in random places to beautify them and attract bees.

When my kids go to a party, we have a chat about goodie bags beforehand. I talk about my view on them (I try my hardest not to make them feel guilty) and say it's totally their choice whether or not they take one. Half the time, they come home with one and, half the time, they don't – I'm totally down with that. Sometimes, my daughter has taken one and, a few days later, she commented that, next time, she'll skip it because everything just ended up in the bin anyway. I don't want my children to be the weird or ungrateful kids at a party – I just want them to be conscious and able to make their own decisions.

Kids' party games

I'll always use what I already have at home for games: egg-and-spoon races, scarves for three-legged races and a pin-the-tail-on-the-donkey drawn on the window are favourites.

Take pass the parcel to the next level by using scarves for wrapping each layer – it not only looks impressive, but the kids find it weirdly exciting.

When it comes to gifts for the winners – we normally roll with something edible or reusable.

Recipe: Seed bombs

YOU WILL NEED

5 parts clay (from your garden, or you can source clay powder from an art supplies shop – just make sure it's pure natural clay)

3 parts compost

2 parts seeds (any kind you like but, ideally, something that grows locally and is relevant to the season)

WHAT TO DO

1. Mix ingredients together, slowly adding water until the mixture is moist and malleable.

2. Roll mixture into golf ball–sized rounds. Dry seed bombs in a warm, sunny spot for 24–48 hours, or until hard.

BUSY TIPS – WHERE TO START?

- Next time you're hosting an event, ask people to bring a plate of food instead of a gift.
- Start making a list on your phone of things your kids (or you) need so you have the ideas at the ready.
- For your next gift, try switching to an experience.

BEING AN ALL–ROUND CONSUMER

'When we try to pick out anything by itself, we find it hitched to everything else in the Universe.' – JOHN MUIR

The way I see it, when it comes to sustainability, consumption is everything. The food we eat, the electricity and water we use, manufacturing that makes the stuff we buy, the waste we generate, our modes of transport – all the things we consume create our impact. When I became aware of one thing, it was a natural progression to start noticing the other impacts I was making.

I started by reducing my toxic load, then I began to create less waste, which moved on to changing my relationship with stuff. Now, I drive an electric car and we've insulated the hell out of our house to reduce our electricity consumption.

It doesn't matter where you start on your pick-a-path adventure, just start somewhere. The rest will unfold as and when it's ready.

If you want inspiration on where to start, you can calculate your carbon footprint. Search for 'carbon calculator' or check futurefit.nz or the Australian Greenhouse calculator from epa.vic.gov.au.

Electricity and water

If we ever build a new home, I would design it as sustainably and efficiently as possible. (Check out the Green Building councils of NZ and Australia for ideas.) I'd choose better over bigger, every time. We live in a home that is nearly 100 years old – everything is on a slight lean and there are cracks and draughts in places there shouldn't be. From an efficiency point of view, it's never going to be perfect, but there are still plenty of things we can do. None of these ideas are breakthrough – it's the way most of us were probably brought up. But I'd slipped into some lazy habits.

Water

I wasn't that big on conserving water until I saw what happened at a wastewater treatment plant. So much energy and resources go into cleaning our water – I had no idea. And then I heard the media about Cape Town nearly running out of drinking water, and something shifted in me – what the hell would we do without clean water? It reconnected me with the value of water and has motivated me to make a few simple changes.

- Fix dripping taps; it saves water and the sound of a dripping tap drives me crazy. If you're waiting for a dripping tap to be fixed, catch the water and use it to water your plants.
- I'm keen to install some rainwater tanks on the house to catch water, then use it on the garden. Or you can use it for drinking water with the right treatment system.
- I will always use the half-flush function on the toilet or, better yet, if you're down with it, only flush when you really need to. Or go all out and get a composting toilet – the innovation in this space is AMAZING.
- We installed a low-flow showerhead. They're really good these days; they use air and water to make sure you don't lose pressure. You can also get shower timers (which I think I will need in my kids' teenage years), or go for a 'navy shower' – get wet, turn off the water, soap up, and then turn on the water to rinse off.
- I clean my car using a bucket of water instead of the hose.
- I'll only use the washing machine or dishwasher when I have a full load.

Electricity

Lights
- Turn off lights when not in use (harder than it sounds when you have husbands and kids in the house).
- Replace with energy-efficient light bulbs (such as LEDs or CFLs). The initial cost outlay can hurt a bit, but they more than pay for themselves over their lifetime. Changing them less often is also a massive win.

Appliances and electronics

- When I'm buying, I look at an appliance's energy- and water-efficiency ratings.
- I'll turn off appliances and electronic gear when they're not in use (sometimes to my husband's sheer frustration).
- We keep appliances well maintained and replace things such as seals on fridges and freezers when we need to.
- We don't have a clothes dryer – but if you do, only use it when you really need to.

Heating

- Get good curtains and make sure your walls, floors and ceilings are as insulated as possible.
- Fill in cracks or use draught stoppers under doors.
- Keep your home well ventilated because damp air is harder to heat – cover pots when cooking, and turn on range hoods and bathroom extraction fans. Also dry your washing outside as much as humanly possible. (I get that this is easier in theory than practice in the middle of winter.)
- I turn off the stovetop a bit early and leave pots on the hot element for food to continue cooking. (We have an electric stovetop.)
- Make the most of your oven heat – often, I don't wait until the oven has fully reached the set temperature before I put things in to start cooking.
- In winter, when I've finished cooking, I turn off the oven and leave the oven door open as it cools down – free heating!
- If you use air-conditioning, try keeping it 1°C cooler in winter and 1°C warmer in summer (and keep the filters clean).

Suppliers

I choose my electricity provider based on their use and development of renewable sources. I'm also looking into getting solar panels installed.

> ⊘ **TIME HACK** A simple way to reduce your impact is making a phone call to switch suppliers.

@ **FIND IT ONLINE** For heaps more tips and advice about energy and water efficiency, check out eeca.govt.nz, energy.gov.au, smartwater.org.nz and smarterhomes.org.nz.

How much do you use?

Before you start reducing your water and electricity usage, check out your latest bills and usage info. You might not notice the impact from turning off lights and using your dryer less initially, but if you start comparing your monthly data, you'll be seriously amazed at the difference you can make (and you'll start saving a heap of cash).

CERTIFICATIONS

Where I can, I support initiatives that are doing their bit to help people make better choices. In a world that's consuming more and more, I'm all for having standards in place that will help to minimise the impact on people and planet. For me, some of the biggies are:

Fair Trade
With a focus on mitigating poverty, Fair Trade is about empowering workers and improving working conditions.

Certified organic
Various certifications exist, but if it contains the words 'certified organic', you're normally on the right track. BioGro and Australian Certified are a couple of the big certifications to look out for locally.

Global Organic Textile Standard (GOTS)
This is a certification that looks at the entire supply chain of a fabric, as well as the treatment of workers.

Marine Stewardship Council (MSC)
This council promotes and certifies sustainable fishing practices and traceability.

Roundtable on Sustainable Palm Oil (RSPO)
This organisation works to promote the growth and use of sustainable oil palm producers. I know palm oil is polarising. The issue is that we are consuming too much of it – my view is that boycotting palm oil will just put pressure on other types of ingredients. Having certifications and programs in place helps us to manage resources better and more sustainably.

Forest Stewardship Council (FSC)
This council promotes the responsible management of the world's forests.

Toitū Envirocare (formerly Enviro-Mark Solutions)
Their Enviro and Carbon marks are awarded to companies, products and services that are taking environmental action.

Certified B Corporations (B Corp)
This group contains companies that are voluntarily meeting high standards when it comes to 'social and environmental performance, public transparency and legal accountability'.

Energy and Water Star Ratings
These rating systems look at the energy and water efficiency of products.

Invite nature in

I've learned to embrace the local biodiversity where I live. Instead of trying to plant a Japanese contemplation garden in the middle of the North Island of New Zealand, I go with native (or edible) plants. Plants grow better and are way easier to maintain, which suits my gardening style (or lack of) way more. Planting natives also attracts some impressive native bird life.

We still have a reasonable amount of lawn but, over time, we're getting more plant life and productive food trees on the go.

> **FIND OUT MORE** Check out treesthatcount.co.nz/ and treesforlife.org.au/ to find out more on how to revegetate your garden with local trees, or to volunteer your time.

We've started renting a beehive – there's a monthly fee and I get free honey in return. While there's a bit of cost involved, I do it because I want to help support the local bee population – they're such a fundamental part of the whole damn ecosystem. I could learn how to keep my own but renting a hive fits where we're at for now.

We have insect hotels and bird feeders to help provide some hospitality for the locals – the kids and the wildlife both love it.

Investment options

We've started making more conscious decisions about where we invest our money. We choose banks and superannuation funds that are investing in sustainable and ethical practices.

> @ **FIND IT ONLINE** Check out responsibleinvestment.org for ideas on responsible and ethical investment providers in Australasia.

BUSY TIPS – WHERE TO START?

- Next time you're in the supermarket look for products with a recognised certification.
- Explore carbon offsetting options. Look for providers that are meeting international standards like ISO 14064. To fully nerd out, check out globalcarbonproject.org.
- Adjust your air conditioner/heater by 1°C.
- → Look back at page 132 to see how we get around and changed to an electric car.

Our rented beehive – all of our neighbours tell us they don't even notice it's there. Just make sure you follow any local council regulations.

The kids aren't running scared! They're totally relaxed around the bees and have only been stung once – when they've accidentally stood on one.

BRINGING OTHERS WITH YOU

'Good company in a journey makes the way seem shorter.' – **IZAAK WALTON**

Your own journey of more mindful consumption might be cranking but, maybe, your family isn't feeling the love, or you're trying to get your work mates on board but Janet in accounting keeps putting her banana skins in the rubbish bin instead of the compost. It sucks feeling like a Lone Ranger, trying to make changes. So how do you bring other people with you – your workmates, family, gym buddies, book club circle or your taxidermy group?

Here are ideas that have worked for me. They're not mutually exclusive and they're not one size fits all. Mix and match – see what sticks.

1. Don't be a dick

This is my number one rule. Too many people in sustainability get all judgey and make other people feel stink about not doing the right thing. Making people feel stink isn't going to inspire change, it's just going to make them feel worse about themselves. They probably won't like you much, either. Everyone is at a different place on their journey; we need to respect that.

I believe in doing what I think is right. People will hopefully notice and, maybe, it will help normalise things for them, or maybe, they'll engage me in conversation and want to know more. (My whole business evolved because I was having so many amazing conversations based on just doing things I thought were right.)

Whenever I take my own container to the sushi shop, at least one other person in the queue will look at what I'm doing and say, 'That's a good idea'. Man, that makes me feel good, because I know there's a chance they'll change their behaviour.

⊘ **TIME HACK** You do you. People will follow.

2. Share your why

Don't be what my friend would call 'rip, sh!t and bust' – you need to bring people with you. Instead of just hitting everyone with a tidal wave of changes at home, in the workplace or anywhere else, providing some context can be useful.

Context helps to explain why you want to make changes and why they're important to you. This can be anything from a casual comment to a family meeting or corporate sustainability vision. Sometimes, it can help if the message comes from someone else . . .

I was waiting for the lift with a colleague named Jo one day; she was telling me how she was an aspiring minimalist, but her husband had sheds full of stuff that he didn't want to get rid of. Jo had tried to talk to him about the benefits of living with less, but he wasn't having a bar of it.

I suggested that, maybe, she could ask him to watch the *Minimalism* documentary.

He wasn't into it, but Jo watched it anyway. Her husband was in and out of the lounge and, obviously, was picking up on things being said. A few days later, he started mentioning how he'd been thinking about the film and that, maybe, it was a good idea to start downsizing his stuff.

3. Know their why

Since changing to only going food shopping every six weeks (→ for the full story, see page 50), we've saved a heap of time. We've been doing this for a few years now but, every few months, my husband will still stand in the kitchen and broadcast how awesome it is that we don't need to spend the next few hours of our weekend shopping for food.

If we're making changes that simplify our lives and save us time, then he's in.

If you know what motivates those around you, tap into that when you're making changes. Money, time, simplification, planet, cool factor – whatever it is, don't judge it, use it. Recognising and harnessing what drives people will mean that your changes will get so much more buy-in and support.

SUSTAINABILITY FILM NIGHT

Watching a movie is an easy way to open people's minds.
Here are some of my favourite documentaries:

- *A Plastic Ocean*
- *An Inconvenient Sequel*
- *The True Cost*
- *2040*
- *Before the Flood*
- *Minimalism*
- *Living the Change: Inspiring Stories
for a Sustainable Future*

Warning – don't watch too many at once! It can get pretty overwhelming.
Just watch enough to drive your 'why', then focus on what you can do,
not how bad things are!

4. Take the path of least resistance

A good friend of mine has a husband who believes recycling is a conspiracy. She
diligently washes and sorts their recycling, but anything not on her watch was
ending up in the rubbish bin.

Instead of getting passive-aggressive about his behaviour (we've all been there),
she simply placed the recycling bin outside the kitchen window. Now it's easier
(and way more fun) to throw any recycling straight out the window. Bending down to
put a bottle in the rubbish bin under the sink can just feel like hard work.

> ⊘ **TIME HACK** Throwing things straight into the recycling bin saves
> time by not double-handling – the bin just gets picked up with the items
> already in it and carried to the kerb for collection. Bloody genius.

When we're trying to influence other people's behaviours, we need to make things
as easy (or fun) as possible. It's about creating the path of least resistance.

- I disconnected my waste disposal unit to avoid the temptation for anyone
  (including me) to use it.
- I moved my veggie garden to be straight outside the kitchen, and in the line
  of sight from the kitchen window. We all now pick things out of the garden
  and weed it way more frequently.
- Set your (and the whole office's) default printer settings to double-sided and
  black-and-white – so simple, but so effective.

> ⊘ **TIME HACK** Understand what's stopping others (be really
> honest, and don't fight it). Now find a way to overcome it.

5. Better together

Parenting has taught me that I get way more buy-in if the kids feel involved in coming up with solutions, instead of me telling them what to do. It's such a simple way to invest people in change.

If something isn't working, or I want to find a better way of doing it, the first thing I now do is have a conversation. It doesn't matter if it's at the family dinner table or the work lunchroom – we all like to be included in decisions.

> ⏱ **TIME HACK** Coming up with solutions together means you don't have to do everything yourself.

Get a buddy

If you're on the journey of making changes, get a buddy to come along for the ride. (No luck in the real world? Join a Facebook group such as Zero Waste in NZ! or Sustainable Living Australia, or use a website like futurefit.nz.) You'll help keep each other motivated and accountable, and you can divide and conquer when researching and trialling solutions.

> **CHALLENGE ACCEPTED!** I met two women who wanted to reduce the amount of stuff they had in their homes – they challenged each other to get rid of a certain number of items each day. Eighteen months later and they've gotten rid of more than 15,000 things!

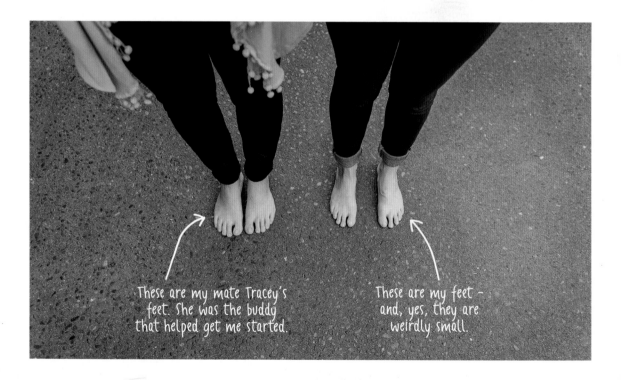

These are my mate Tracey's feet. She was the buddy that helped get me started.

These are my feet – and, yes, they are weirdly small.

THE FINAL WORD

Running into an ex-colleague one day, he mentioned he was surprised I was still going with this whole 'sustainability fad'. After laughing awkwardly, it got me thinking ... after the novelty of reading a book or making a couple of changes has worn off, how do you stay motivated? How do you keep going?

Why, oh, why
The single best thing I've done to keep on track has been knowing my 'why' and making changes that are in line with it. If I'm saving time, improving my family's wellbeing and lightening my impact, I'll never look back.

Change feels good
As humans we will do things that make us feel good. I get a little buzz every time I do something that lessens my impact, or if someone else comments positively about what I'm doing. It's that feel-good factor – I'm a little bit hooked on it.

Measure your results
I love having tangible results, so I know where I'm at. Money and time saved, waste reduced, how little you buy new – whatever fits with your why, measure it. It's easy to lose track of how far you've come, so this is a sure-fire way to keep you going. ←

'What gets measured gets done.'

Celebrate your wins
Anytime I sell something, the money goes into a separate 'good times' account. We use that money for family holidays and other fun things. I also make sure that the time we save from not going shopping is spent doing fun stuff together as a family.

One small change at a time
We're human and we're busy – tackle one thing at a time. Trying to change everything at once will just end up overwhelming you and those around you. Everyone knows the story of the hare and the tortoise – it doesn't matter how slowly you move forward, as long as you're moving.

Keep it real.
Nic

THANKS

This whole book-writing gig is pretty full on. It's been a hell of a journey and I want to give a shout out to some of the awesome humans who have helped me along the way. You've all let me bounce ideas off you, looked after my kids or just backed me and what I do.

There are sooo many more people that have shaped things: to every single one of you, I'm sending a virtual high five – thanks heaps!

Tori Veysey Maree McNulty + Amber Bremner Mama and Pard Sally Fraser
Geoff Wallace All of the awesome case study contributors Becs Jones
Liz Burrett Charlotte Catmur Mike and the kids
Tim Carter Kristina Peina Nan + Poppa Andrea Twaddle Megan van Staden Debbie Harrison
Grandad and China Liss Oliver Alex Hedley
Chris & the girls Caro Izzard Charlotte Isaac Becks Tosswill Sarah McCullagh Kaye Olsen
Meraki workspace Jane Coxhead
Barbara McClenahan Tracey Cameron Amanda Hema
Kirsty Quickfall #reducetogrow
Anna Harnden-Taylor All of my social media supporters

SOURCES ← Cool people and organisations that were my go-tos for info.

storyofstuff.org
UNenvironment.org
lovefoodhatewaste.co.nz
OzHarvest.org
ellenmacarthurfoundation.org

drawdown.org
worldwildlife.org
truecostmovie.com
creativebrainmovie.com

Ewg.org
Chemicalmaze.com
Davidsuzuki.org
Figgyandco.co.nz